D1599947

The OLD HOME PLACE

Farming on the West Texas Frontier

Howard County Library

Big Spring, Texas

Presented by

1905 Hyperion Club

In Memory of

Mr. J.C. Pickle

Howard County Library
Big Spring, Texas

976.473
C116

The OLD HOME PLACE

Farming on the West Texas Frontier

David L. Caffey

Eakin Press • Burnet, Texas

Howard County Library
Big Spring, Texas

071790

The map on the front and back
end sheets was originally published
in 1884 by A. & C. Black, Edinburgh.
It is reproduced here courtesy of
The Southwest Collection,
Texas Tech University.

Copyright © 1981
By David L. Caffey

Published in the United States of America
By Eakin Press, P.O. Drawer AG, Burnet, Texas 78611

ALL RIGHTS RESERVED

ISBN 0-89015-283-7

CONTENTS

*   *   *

Maps

Maps prepared by
Keith Bratton

vi

Introduction

There are places in the world where one can hardly travel without being struck by a profound and immediate sense of history—places where medieval castles, colonial buildings, fine old homes, or the ruins of ancient dwellings and places of worship bring times long past to life before the eyes and ears of the present.

West Texas is not that kind of place. Across the miles of West Texas, there is not much to remind the casual passerby that the region has much of a past at all. Many events that might have been of historical interest were ones that left no trace. There is not much to see about a stage line or cattle trail that once crossed the prairie, or about a site where nomadic Indians pitched their lodges for a time before moving on to better hunting.

When white settlers first came to the prairie, they built plain log and board dwellings—structures not calculated to survive many years of fires, wind, and West Texas weather. Eventually, more substantial homes and public buildings were raised, and some of the early ones have lasted to the present day, but in many more cases, the developing cities have displayed an unfortunate penchant for tearing down the older structures to make way for new ones. The consequence is a landscape dominated by the present, one with few relics to demand recognition of the past.

But there was, even in the short century since the coming of white pioneers, another era and another time when things were fundamentally different, when another way of living prevailed and thrived. To find its traces, one must take to the backroads and byways, search for faded signs of the older era along the dusty farm roads and fencelines. Mainly, there are three hints of the older time to be found across the forgotten stretches of the older West Texas counties. These are: the vacant country school buildings, small rural churches, and the weathered, leaning walls of long abandoned farmhouses.

For every one of these structures that remains, many others have vanished entirely, their plots now overgrown with weeds and mesquite trees. For now, the few that remain only give silent testimony to a time when the rural countryside was sprinkled liberally with such structures, and with the people who made and used them. They are from an era when most people lived on the land, when large families lived on small farms of eighty to one hundred and sixty acres, when rural communities were bound close around the small country schools and churches. This pattern was characteristic of a way of life that lasted from the settling of the farming frontier until the economic collapse of the small cotton farms—roughly from the 1880s to the Great Depression. To portray that era is the aim of this book.

My grandfather and his three brothers all came to be part of the era of "the old home place" in Jones County, Texas. All of the brothers were born in the hills of northern Mississippi in the years just before and after the Civil War, and eventually all of them moved west to the developing farming frontier. All four lived most of their adult lives fashioning small farms out of the native shinnerylands of Jones County and living off those farms, and all of the men came finally to be buried in the same cemetery on a low knoll out east from Anson, Texas.

Like so many others, these men and their families came from poor lives in the old southern states to look for better times in the expansive climate of the new western territories. The abundance of cheap land played no small part in bringing them west. The new country that they found filled in and grew up in a pattern of rural communities scattered around the small towns that supported the farming enterprise. The four brothers from Mississippi thus were part of a pattern and a way of life that lasted only so long, and then ceased to exist. Their story illustrates and, to some degree, typifies the experiences of many others who lived through the early decades of the farm frontier.

The story related here is intended as a true account, and although it is not presented as a formal history, every event and person is as made known to me by some particular source. Much of the material comes from the recollections of people who experienced the times and events firsthand. Some of it comes from courthouse records and legal documents, some from personal papers and newspaper files. Some of it is hearsay. None of it is "made up."

Occasionally friends have heard me speak of the home place and of my efforts to comprehend and then to portray the era. Some of them have, correctly I suppose, detected a certain nostalgic affection for the old days on my part. Sometimes I am asked, "Do you think it was a better time? Was life better then?"

Well, I don't know about that. I am hesitant to advance an absolute, all encompassing judgement on the merits of that era or any other. But, I do believe that it was better in this way: Children grew up closer to the natural earth and had an easier time understanding their place in relation to the other elements of the natural world. Birth and death occurred close at hand, were less mysterious and more easily accepted as natural aspects of life. The link between human needs and the earth's resources was likewise more direct, more easily recognized. Food, fuel, shelter, and clothing did not come pre-manufactured and pre-packaged and pre-processed through the unseen channels of a complex market economy; rather, these things were substantially produced at home and out of the resources of the land itself.

Moreover, children of the old family farms perhaps grew up with a sense of self worth that is less common among young people now. Children of the industrial age often seem to be defeated by the very systems and conveniences that have made their lives easier. Time consuming chores of the older days have largely been reduced to the flip of a switch or the press of a button, leaving many of the young to the hollow search for "something to do" and for some point to life beyond sheer existence. In the older era, field work, wood cutting, and hog killing provided "something to do," and provided even the young child with a way of achieving the satisfaction of contributing directly to his own sustenance. Whatever the merits of the new age, a great many among its people have been so well provided for by systems that they are left without worthwhile work to do, without the natural means for affirming their own worth.

Several acknowledgments are set forth elsewhere in this book. But it is fair to say here that the book could not have been if not for my father, Wiley Caffey. Though he was no longer living when the book was conceived, his influence nonetheless went a long way in causing it to be written. My father grew up on the home place and his conversation was full of references to his growing up years. He told dozens of stories about his boyhood times and, without trying to, he put across the sense and the flavor of the time and place that he knew as a boy. Although he never received a diploma or degree, my father went on from the country schools to attend college and law school, and to serve as County Judge and District Attorney for Taylor County, Texas. He was, in addition, as thoroughly honest and unpretentious as anyone I have known.

Finally, I owe a special debt of gratitude to Mrs. Helen DeVitt Jones of Lubbock, Texas. Mrs. Jones became interested in the manuscript and offered financial support that opened the way to its publication. Moreover, her genuine and persisting interest in the project was a source of extreme personal gratification and encouragement.

David L. Caffey

1. The Old Country

Not many people remember Shady Grove, where my grandfather, Mart Caffey, grew up. Not that there is much to remember. Shady Grove was never more than a one room school and a country church and an indistinct community of hill country farmers in the tall woods of northeastern Mississippi—an obscure place where nothing much ever happened, save for the turning of the seasons and the everyday lives of plain country people.

But Shady Grove is where the tale of the home place begins, at least as far as I know it. Certainly the chain of circumstances and events that brought my family to West Texas stretches backward into the ages quite far enough to boggle the imagination. But before Shady Grove, I am forever lost in a tangle of begats and spelling quandaries and census records—not the stuff of stories. It is only with Shady Grove and the Civil War years that figures emerge from the haze that old tintypes and tales remembered give shape and substance to the people and events of a personal heritage.

I have been to Shady Grove, or to what's left of it. I have sometimes wondered whether I would ever have found it, had I not by chance met up with Mr. Johnny Gardner, proprietor of the store at Wheeler, Mississippi. Tall and lean and ripe with years, Mr. Johnny laughed easily and remembered much. He remembered the chestnut trees that grew thick over the countryside in his boyhood years, before the blight that took them all. He remembered the little church at Hodges Chapel—how it looked and how it was situated in the little clearing. He remembered the way to old Shady Grove, and he led me there across the winding backroads. In time, I found a farm and a tumbledown cabin, a churchyard and two weathered headstones, and a country as green and peaceful as any I have known. I found, too, some of the origins of the home place, and of myself.

Shady Grove is barely a place at all any more. The school is long gone, the white frame church no longer standing. There are still people and houses among the hills and hollows and high crowned oak trees, but no one seems to speak of the Shady Grove community nowadays. Some of the residents do not know that the place has such a name. The people now take divergent paths, many of them to the factories around Booneville and Corinth. There is no central institution or feature to bring them together, or to give the place a current identity. It is not even marked on the present day county road map. About the only evidence of a place called Shady Grove is the churchyard cemetery in a clearing where the church house stood.

*   *   *

Since 1870 the Shady Grove country has been part of Prentiss County, but before then it was still part of old Tishomingo County, which was organized just after Mississippi was opened to eastern settlers and which took in the whole northeastern corner of the new state. In the years just preceding the Civil War, my great grandfather John T. Caffey was among the farmers who labored over small patches of farmland in the Tishomingo hills. He and the others cultivated the bottomlands in a primitive fashion, using mules and homemade implements to raise cotton and food crops.

When rumors of war were first passed among the hill folk, John was at his usual work, bringing his crops along through the late summer months. With the eventual election of Lincoln and the resulting wave of secession conventions across the South, the talk grew more serious. When

2

Mississippi took up the question, Tishomingo County sent its delegates south to Jackson. The Tishomingo men took a moderate stance on the matter of secession, but the hot-bloods prevailed, and Mississippi left the Union immediately. With the question settled and troops to be raised, the county provided its share, and then some.

When the enlistment call first went out, my great grandfather didn't go. He stayed on his own land and went about his work. Before many months, the war would come to him.

Over the early months of the conflict, battles and skirmishes were indecisive, but as the two sides settled in for a long struggle, Union forces began their gradual penetration of the South, bringing the war ever nearer the Tishomingo people. As 1861 ended, Buell and Grant were driving Union armies southward through Kentucky and Tennessee. As they advanced across Tennessee and made their way toward Mississippi, Bragg and Beauregard brought Confederate troops forward to meet them.

Before long the paths of advance and retreat ran through the hills of Tishomingo. Confederate and Union troops often marched through Booneville, each side periodically plotting some new maneuver designed to secure the advantage appertaining to the critical junction of two main railroads at the town of Corinth, twenty miles to the north and just below the Tennessee line. In May of 1862 Union soldiers raided the Mobile and Ohio at Booneville, burned the station house and set fire to sixty freight wagons. By July, fifteen to twenty thousand federal troops were camped in Tuscumbia bottom, between Booneville and Corinth. By mid-October the Union had taken control of the rails, sent the rebel army limping southward beaten and bleeding.

In November Major Lowry passed through Tishomingo seeking to muster new recruits and shore up the sagging Confederate effort. John T. Caffey, thirty years old at the time, signed up for the standard enlistment of ''three years or the war.'' Why he waited until this time to take up the cause, or why he now chose to do so, I do not know. It may be that, with his crops in and a conscription law recently passed by the Southern congress, he felt compelled to join in. I do know that he left behind in the hills of Tishomingo a wife, Nancy; a six year old boy, Edgar; and the freshly covered grave where he and Nancy had only recently buried a four year old daughter. John mustered into the 32nd Mississippi Infantry, marched across Tennessee and fought the yankees at Murfreesboro.

That the war produced greater carnage and more casualties among Americans than any event before or since is widely recognized. The horrors of the battlefield have been well understood, but what is often overlooked is the extent of suffering and devastation that took place behind the front lines. Open latrines, spoiled food supplies, and haphazard use of water sources left many camps filthy and disease ridden. Food shortages and unsanitary living conditions too often rendered the troops weak, demoralized, and vulnerable to sickness. A great many soldiers were lost in combat, but many others lost their lives in vain and ignominious ways—died of typhoid or diptheria or acute dysentery brought on by the miserable circumstances of the battle camps. In July of his first full year in the army, John fell sick and was taken to the makeshift military hospital at Chattanooga. There he lay through the summer, fall, and winter, never growing much better or worse.

Had John married a girl more like himself—affable, agreeable, easygoing—he might well have died in Chattanooga to be buried by some indifferent fellow traveler in a vast field of identical battlefield graves. But the fact of the matter was that Nancy was not at all like her husband in grit and temperament. Possessions were not important to John; whatever a neighbor asked, he would gladly have given. Not so his wife; Nancy didn't covet material things either, but she carried a stubborn sense of right that made her stick up for her way time and again, regardless how small or large the substance of an issue. Where her husband was apt to be charitable and conciliatory, Nancy

4

didn't mince words. When she took offense, she said so in plain terms and clear tones that left no one in doubt.

When Nancy had not heard from her husband for several months, she went asking after him in town. When she learned what had happened, she took Edgar and the wagon and made the two hundred mile journey overland to Chattanooga. She found John wasted with sickness and hunger. She hauled him back across Tennessee to the familiar hills of home, fed him up and cared for him until he was well again. When John saw that he would recover, he made a promise to the Almighty. For the rest of his years he would preach the Gospel and do the Lord's work in the hills south of Booneville.

*   *   *

The northern Mississippi country was a land of hills and hollows, twists and turns. With the rolling terrain and the high crowned hardwood forest that covered most of it, it was a country of small, secluded places. Each bend in the road left one scene behind, revealed a new glade or valley. Nestled in among the trees were quiet clearings like the ones in which the churches stood. Hidden away, too, were natural meadows protected and secluded by the woodlands. Along many of the creeks were narrow strips of bottomland cleared from the sideslopes along the streambeds.

The land was rich, and at the same time poor. It was rich in beauty and in the green foliage that seemed to grow everywhere, the product of moderate temperatures, fine textured soils, and a rainy wet climate. Beneath the pine and the high topped oak forest were lesser stands of ash, maple, and sumac. Among the trees grew the tangle of greenbriar, Virginia creeper, and the white blossomed honeysuckle. In summer a lush fullness came over the countryside, everywhere in shades of green. So wet was the country and so fast growing the greenery that a tumbledown shed or pen abandoned for only a season or two soon was overgrown and claimed for quaintness and antiquity.

For all the beauty of the green rolling country, it was poor in its productive capacity, and the families of the rural countryside were hard pressed to wring a meager living from it. Crop lands were scarce, wedged into shallow, open hollows or lying in narrow, ambling ribbons that followed the gentle slopes along the creeks. In some places a chain of small meadows could be strung together by clearing off the level woodlands that separated them. The country people had heard of places where crops lay all around in a flat, level expanse that extended for miles to a distant horizon, but the Prentiss County farms were not that way. Each farmer pieced together his crop lands from the odd shaped patches that could be fitted into the low places of the rolling country. A man might work several patches, each a few acres, in order to raise his crops.

Where land could be cleared and cultivated, a certain amount of pampering was required to keep it tillable and productive. The places that were level enough for cultivation generally lay in the bottomlands, along the drainage or in a low valley. What with the generous rains that came to northern Mississippi, the low places were almost constantly saturated or under water unless pains were taken to drain them. Where the natural creeks and waterways were insufficient for this purpose, farmers dug their own ditches that carried off the excess waters and divided the lands into still smaller plots. In an unusually wet year the lower edges of the cleared plots were too boggy to be worked very effectively, but in a dry year they produced the best crops of all.

There was one more problem with the crop lands. They were worn down from forty years of giving up their potency to one cotton crop after another. Certainly it was still possible to produce a stand of cotton plants each year, and to harvest mature bolls in the fall, but they weren't the hearty plants and bountiful, full sprung bolls the farmers had seen in earlier years, when the land was new. Much of the soil's fertility had been sapped away, and it could only be revived by a cumbersome and expensive process of adding manure, and even then the effects were short lived. The situation was to some extent the result of ignorance to sound principles of agriculture, but it was also due to the farmers' inclination to plant the one familiar money crop year after year. To some, the increasing impotency of the soil mattered little. When the land no longer gave up a decent harvest, they would move on to new ground that had yet to be turned.

Even after the country had been settled and the patches of tillable land cleared, most of northern Mississippi lay in the shade. With its dark, wooded places, hidden clearings, and farm places secluded away among the hills and hollows, it was good country for one who loved solitude. It shut out the bustle of towns and rails, kept troublesome affairs of the larger society out of sight and out of mind. Here a man could graze on his thoughts, could muse on the verities of life and move through the seasons at a leisurely, unhurried pace. Life was slow.

*   *   *

When the war was over and for nearly thirty years after, John Caffey raised cotton and ministered to the people of south Prentiss County. Through the week he worked his own patches of bottomland, busting the ground behind a mule and single row plow, working his way along with a shovel to fashion and clean drainage ditches. When he was needed at some cabin across the countryside, he dropped his work and went to help. On Sundays, he rode his circuit ahorseback, making the rounds of the rural community churches at Shady Grove and Meadow Creek and Hodges Chapel. Over the rolling hills he rode—a red headed preacher on a chestnut horse—through the patches of bottomland and beneath the great oaks and native pine that spread their billowing canopy over the hillsides.

John and Nancy finally reared four sons in all, the boys born over a span of nineteen years. Edgar was the oldest by ten years. Oscar came along shortly after the war, in 1866. Three years later came the birth of my grandfather, Martin Luther, called "Mart." Fletcher, the last of the four, was born in 1875.

The family lived around on several different pieces of farmland over John's forty years in the country near Booneville. Throughout most of Mart's boyhood, up until he was fourteen, they lived on an eighty acre farm next to the Bennett place, a mile west of Meadow Creek Church and that far to the south of Hodges Chapel. During these years Mart grew up alongside Abb Bennett, the neighbor boy, and the two became fast friends for life, though one would stay in the Mississippi hills and one would strike out for new country.

In 1883 John paid four hundred dollars for a quarter section of land a few miles to the east, over in the broad valley that lay between Meadow Creek and the low ridge that hid Shady Grove. John soon sold half the land, but he and Nancy settled in on the eighty acres that they kept, and there they lived out their lives.

The new home was on Casey Creek. That it appeared as a neat rectangle on the county clerk's map went against the whole character of the land, for the country did not lend itself naturally to squared off plots. It rolled and rambled in a fanciful way, the open strips running away to the low places in playful crooks and bulges, the wooded ridges dividing the country into ravines and hollows instead of sections. John's cabin was of squared logs, boards, and shake shingles. It stood at the head of a shallow valley and faced out over the cleared patches that fell away to the east. The cabin was set back into the recess of the valley's tapered upper end, woodlands encircling behind and along both sides of the crop lands. Of John's eighty acres, the few cleared patches made up perhaps thirty acres, which the preacher worked with a hand forged plowshare, handmade harness, and mules. Down through the clearing trickled the shallow, overgrown waters of Casey Creek. Tall grasses and willow saplings grew alongside, dividing the cultivated plots to either side.

When there was trading to do, the folks around Shady Grove journeyed six miles north, to Booneville. In the town were the usual shops and offices, schools and churches. After Tishomingo was split into four counties following the war, the courthouse for Prentiss County also came to be placed in Booneville. In the late 1850s the Mobile and Ohio tracks had been laid through town, and thereafter there was direct passenger and freight traffic north and south. For many years the daily spectacle in Booneville was "train time," twenty-two minutes past twelve, when both the one northbound and the one southbound passenger train passed through Booneville, causing a flurry at the depot. The Prentiss *Recorder* published news to the county on a weekly basis, and later the *Pleader* and the Prentiss *Plaindealer* took its place.

Protestant fundamentalism ran deep in the rural country of northern Mississippi. The country churches, small and plain as they might have appeared, were for the most part strong and active. Each was the central institution of its community—the binding force among the country people and the source of occasions for coming together.

Southern Baptists were strong in the region, with Methodists close behind and a fair representation of Presbyterians in evidence. Singings and socials and revivals were commonplace at all of the churches, of whatever persuasion and whatever size. Children were given weekly instruction from the Bible, encouraged to memorize verses and strive for the small prizes that were given to reward diligent study.

That the country churches flourished is undoubtedly due in part to the lack of any other social attraction. But it is also perhaps indicative of the extent to which the faith was real to a great many of the rural people. For many of them religion was not a part-time thing, but an integral element in their everyday lives. At home John's boys were taught to study the Bible and to regard it as a source of authority to be accepted and obeyed, not only to be read, but to be understood in relation to everyday happenings and experiences. It was not something to be questioned. Nancy followed and enforced the Sabbath day in her own strict way. All of her cooking and household chores were done on Saturday, so that Sunday meals could be served without undue effort or distraction. Any other day the boys were free to roam the hills and seek out their playmates on neighboring farms, but on Sunday they went to church and then spent the rest of the day around home.

John's ministry was not a very formal affair. He wasn't an ordained conference member who moved from one town pulpit to another and perhaps carried aspirations of becoming a bishop. Rather he was a Methodist "service preacher," who stayed on his own land, rode the circuit, and kept the rural churches going year after year. Many of the hill people were barely getting by. They had little money with which to pay the preacher, so John more often rode in home with a towsack thrown over his saddle—the sack bulging with canned goods or jerking to the noisy squabbles of a pair of hens given him by one of the neighbors.

Preaching services were carried off with a miminum of stiffness. Given the intimate and homey settings in which they took place, it could hardly have been otherwise. As with the other chapels, Shady Grove Church stood in a deep and peaceful clearing, bounded close around by the high woodlands. The church sat on the highest ground in the little glade, with the churchyard and its few headstones falling away toward the trees. The building had two front doors a few feet apart, corresponding to two narrow aisles that separated the columns of hard wooden benches. Along each side were plain windows that could be opened to provide light and ventilation, and behind the pulpit were two windows that could be propped open to make a breeze in the sultry days of summer.

On one summer Sunday, John stood preaching to his congregation while outside the dogs ran loose and raised a howl. John's young boy Fletcher sat along one of the side aisles, bored and fidgety as he waited for the sermon to be over. Fletcher was but nine or ten years old, but already he had the mischievous streak that would remain a part of his character for life. Having nothing better to do, Fletcher leaned out the window and snapped his fingers, caught the dogs' attention and set them on two goats grazing in the clearing. Soon the dogs and goats were engaged in a lively romp as the dogs gave chase round and round the chapel. The dogs crowded close on the heels of the poor harried goats, and finally on one turn around the church house, one of the goats turned in through an open door, fled down the aisle, bolted past the pulpit, and exited in a fit of panic through the open window behind the preacher.

The rural communities barely had schools at all. There wasn't the money for good buildings and trained teachers, so the country people got by the best they could with plain schoolrooms, part-time teachers, and shared schoolbooks. Edgar missed out to some extent, growing through childhood as he did, during the chaotic war years. Mart and Fletcher, the two younger boys, had a more normal experience in the country schools, and they came to be reasonably well educated, for their circumstances. Northern Mississippi, for its backwardness in other ways, had a few boarding schools where classical learning was valued and upheld. The academies at Booneville and Jacinto provided instruction in Latin, Greek, and classical literature, in addition to the basic three Rs. Some of their influence fell over onto the public and rural schools, so that even the children of the hill country farmers came to be exposed to prose and poetry of some of the revered authors of all time. Though the school terms scarcely ran over four months, it was possible for a boy to learn not only to read and write, but to appreciate a cleverly turned thought or a good story as well.

*   *   *

Aside from their parents, there was one person who influenced the boys' lives more than any other. That per-

071720   Howard County Library
Big Spring, Texas

son was their grandfather, Miles Thomas. Miles Thomas had been one of the first white settlers in Mississippi, had helped organize the society and had remained one of the leaders in south Prentiss County. He was an instigator and a man of considerable civic involvement wherever he went. During his lifetime, he helped organize counties, schools, and churches, not once, but in several different places in the course of his periodic moves from one locality to another.

It is likely that Miles Thomas provided some of the encouragement for his grandsons in their pursuit of school-ing. What is more certain is that he had much to do with their willingness, as grown young men, to strike out in pursuit of unseen country.

When the dust from the war years had settled and westward expansion could proceed again, rumors trickled eastward telling of unoccupied lands available in the western territories. Not so very far off was the boundless expanse of western Texas—of promising virgin farmlands that could be had at low cost. The territory was by now politically secure, but virtually empty of white settlers. Migration to the frontier, once stymied because of the war, and then because of the presence of hostile Indians, now began in earnest. With newcomers stopping in the nearest counties where lands were available, the line of settlement gradually advanced across the eastern half of Texas. By the mid-seventies, Wise County, in north central Texas, was part of the forward region now soaking up landseekers and offering them hopes of more prosperous lives in a new land.

The talk of migration to the opening Texas country, the promise of a golden opportunity, the prospect of in-volvement in a new society—these touched off the truest and most fundamental impulses in Miles Thomas, in-vigorated his aging bones and set him figuring and dealing and calculating, selling off the properties of one life and planning for another. With some of his kin attached to the enterprise, he packed up the accumulated belongings of forty years in Mississippi, and hauled them west.

Two years later, in 1878, Edgar Caffey was a twenty-two year old man with a wife and infant son. Following the path that his grandfather Thomas had taken, Edgar left his father and mother, the three younger boys who were his brothers, and the country of green hills and high tree tops, and set off to find his future in Wise County, Texas.

2. Two Faces West

The ever advancing frontier was, for several generations, the salvation of many an American family. With new territories opening up continually over the several decades of westward expansion and settlement, even children of the poor could foster hopes of a dignified life in which honest work, property ownership, and prosperity were possible. This is not to say that the pioneering life would be easy, or that it was certain to be rewarding. The life was almost never easy, and many were the pilgrimages of young couples that began in hope and ended in frustration, failure, or tragedy. Some tried the new lands for a time, grew discouraged and went back where they had come from. Still, there were undeniable possiblities for those who were free, white, and willing to uproot themselves and grapple with unknown obstacles in an unfamiliar and hostile place.

For many families, this meant that children, even several of them, might hope to prosper on the cheap lands and open horizons of a developing frontier society. The cycle in which poverty is passed from one generation to the next was perhaps not nearly so strong as it had been in earlier years, or as it would be again in later times. The son or daughter of the frontier era was not so dependent on the family's holdings for future prospects. During the expansion years, the new generation could maintain the accustomed style of living by moving to new country where inexpensive lands were available in abundance. Thus there were families where this move to the newest frontier occurred not once, but again and again.

Mart Caffey came from such a family. His grandfather Michael Caffey had come from North Carolina in 1836, in the first years of settlement by whites in western Tennessee; Mart's own father had made that trek as a four year old boy. Michael's father and grandfather had come to the sparsely settled Carolinas from Maryland shortly after the American Revolution. And before them was an Irish linen maker, Michael Caffey, who had left the land of his birth to sail for the American colonies. Mart's other grandfather, Miles Thomas, was one of the earliest white settlers to enter northern Mississippi following the Treaty of Pontotoc and the removal of the Chickasaws westward to the Indian Territory. By Mart's tenth birthday, Miles had left for yet another frontier in Texas, with Edgar following close behind.

During all the years of Mart's youth, new territories continued to be opened up for settlement. Yet to be peopled after the Civil War was the great expanse beyond the Missouri. The process was to consume most of four decades. Through various schemes of dispersement, huge areas were turned over to hopeful pioneers in 160 acre parcels. The Homestead Act provided for the free distribution of western lands, with incentives for the kinds of permanent improvements that would ensure the organized presence of white Americans in the territories. Later the railroads became trustees of large holdings of western lands granted to them by the government as a relatively painless way of subsidizing and stimulating the construction of cross-continental railways. The railroads then undertook distribution of these lands, many of which were sold for farms and townsites. As quickly as the buffalo could be exterminated and the Indians subdued, settlers moved in.

If the frontier meant salvation for the generations of young easterners, it meant tragedy for as many generations of American Indians. It is mind boggling to think of the transformation that had to take place between the war and 1900—between the time nomadic tribes could be seen following massive herds of buffalo and the time when the lands would be fenced and farmed and the Indians excluded altogether from all but a fraction. Settlers found the go-

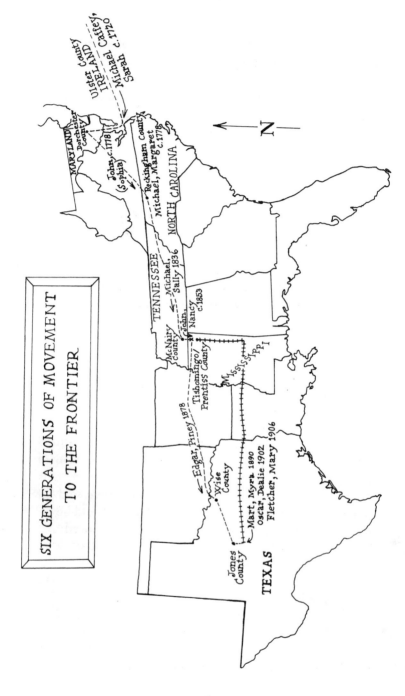

SIX GENERATIONS OF MOVEMENT
TO THE FRONTIER

Ulster County
IRELAND   Michael Caffey,
Sarah c.1720

MARYLAND
Dorchester
County

John, c.1778
(Sophia)

Rockingham County
Michael, Margaret
c.1778

NORTH CAROLINA

TENNESSEE

Michael,
Sally 1836

McNairy
County

John,
Nancy
c.1853

Tishomingo/
Prentiss County

M
I
S
S
I
S
S
I
P
P
I

Edgar, Piney 1878

Wise
County

Mart, Myra 1890
Oscar, Dealie 1902
Fletcher, Mary 1906

Jones
County

TEXAS

N

ing rough and slow in the years just after Appomattox, but once the government could be persuaded of the necessity for using military force, the U.S. Army overpowered the plains tribes quickly and efficiently.

When Mart turned twenty-one in the spring of 1889, there was still open country, cheap land, and the rumor of opportunity on the farming frontier of the west. New lands were yet coming open, though by this time most of them were to be found in small, tightly contained pockets that were well known to homeseekers and that had been held out from settlement for a particular reason. Many of these were Indian lands that had come to be more compulsively sought as the public homestead lands ran out. A focus of the clamor was the Indian Territory of Oklahoma, where a relatively few Indians clung to stretches of desirable lands in a system of common ownership that the white man found inscrutable. After several years of agitation on the frontier and dickering in Congress, a vast part of the Indian Territory was declared open to homestead settlement. A month after Mart's twenty-first birthday came the somewhat sensational news of thousands of landseekers massed on the boundary of the homestead land, and of the reckless scramble that followed. Even in backwoods Mississippi they heard about the land rush and knew people who had gone there.

Of more lasting interest to a young man looking for a move was the Texas farming frontier, where lands were not free, but cheap and plentiful. Here were dozens of counties of central and west Texas lands desirable for farming—platted off into counties, available for distribution to settlers, but sparsley populated for want of new settlers. For years settlement had been held up because of the resistance of Comanches and Kiowas, but in the early 1870s U.S. troops were loosed on the tribes, and by 1875 all but the stragglers had been defeated, removed, confined. Buffalo still roaming the plains in large numbers were marked for extinction, not only because they gave sustenance to the Indian way of life, but because the unruly buffalo made their own menace to farmers and stockmen as well. Conveniently, the market for hides was prosperous, and once the northern herds had been exhausted, hunters turned southward to the herds of the Texas plains. The years 1875 to 1878 were boom years for the buffalo hunters, as hides were shipped eastward by the hundreds of thousands. By 1880, the buffalo were gone, and with them the last impediment to settlers.

As the hazards receded, settlement followed. By 1876 immigrants were entering Texas in droves, the Thomases and all the rest. Year by year the line of settlement edged westward. When Mart's grandfather Thomas moved into Wise County in 1876, he was at the leading edge of settlement, but by 1880 the surrounding counties had filled in and the influx of new settlers looked farther west.

By 1882 railroads had pushed through Texas, through the farmlands and beyond into the deserts of far western Texas. Settlement quickly proceeded to the western limits of arable lands along the railroad routes, then followed more slowly in areas outland from the rail lines. Available at bargain prices were vast acreages of public domain, school lands, and railroad holdings. Unlike the homestead regions farther north, many of these lands were bought in large tracts, often at public auction, by individuals or development companies, who then divided them into rent farms or sold them to farmers in smaller parcels. Whether owned by state or investor, it took settlers to make the land pay. An open invitation and the promise of maximum opportunity for minimum cash investment brought the homeseekers in a steady stream until each part of the farmlands had been occupied and developed from county line to county line.

Many of those heading for the West Texas farm country came from states in the old South. The traces to Texas had been long established, ever since slaveholders had moved into east Texas, into country much like the country of the old South, to create a plantation society that resembled those of the southern coastal states. Cotton and corn and hogs and cattle made up the economic base. Baptists, Methodists, and Presbyterians predominated among the churchgoing people as they had back in the older states. After Reconstruction and during the years of westward settlement across Texas, the path from the southern states continued familiar and natural to farmers of modest means and ambitious appetites. In most of the West Texas counties of the 1890s it would have been possible to ask around about the origins of each family and find that a good many had come from Arkansas, Tennessee, Mississippi, Georgia, Alabama, and perhaps from as far as the Carolinas. It was in an environment of rumored opportunity in a far off country, of hopes aroused and the sudden departures of neighbors and acquaintances, that Mart Caffey grew to manhood on the shaded little farm in backwoods Mississippi.

It is doubtful whether any of the facts about the westward movement or about his own family's particular pioneering heritage mattered much to Mart. What mattered a great deal more were his plans to marry Samyrah Lollar and his wish that they might someday have something of their own. Edgar had now been in Texas twelve years, and still there came the rumors of cheap and plentiful lands—fertile places where a man and wife willing to work might soon buy into a place of their own. Mart's prospects in Mississippi were sorry, or at least uninteresting, compared to the visions of broad, open farmlands, bustling new towns, and fairly rapid progress toward ownership.

When Mart became serious about moving west, he corresponded with his older brother concerning the possibilities. Edgar had lately come to be interested in Jones County, which lay to the west of Wise County and farther into the western reaches of Texas. Jones County still evidenced the raw qualities of the frontier, still offered many of its advantages and drawbacks. It was said to be a place with a good and prosperous future. While land prices in Wise County had crept upward with the saturation of

19

new settlers and the maturation of a second generation from the older settlers, Jones County still had more land than people. Much of Jones County was covered with a blackjack and post oak growth that ranged from scruffy to the size of a mature tree stunted only by a lack of abundant water. The land was level, though, and could be cleared until a farmer had attained the desired balance between open field for crops and wooded land for pasture.

The good people of Jones County did nothing to stem the hopes of the far-away dreamers contemplating a move to the frontier. Each enterprising new county or settlement had its promoters who actively practiced to attract newcomers. At about the time Mart was making his move, several of the county's most ardent and artful boosters prepared to publish the first issue of their promotional bulletin: *Jones County, Texas; A Monthly Publication for Home-Seekers.* The paper appeared in the early months of 1891, just after Mart had located in the county. The prospective settler was tempted with the promise of good land—any kind he might choose:

> "Do you want a rich black sandy loam? We have it. Do you want a rich chocolate soil? It is here. Do you want highly fertile red soil? We have plenty of it here. Do you want black prairie land? There is plenty of it here. Do you want river bottom, valley land, table land, smooth level prairie, heavily timbered or open prairie land? You can find all of these in Jones County. We have the finest lands that can be found in Texas."

> "West Texas is the best part of the State, and Jones County is the garden spot of the West."

The publication addressed the sundry concerns of the curious reader.

. . . Comfort:

"No sir; Jones County is not out on the plains where they burn Buffalo chips for fuel. We have plenty of timber for fuel and fencing purposes. . . . No danger of freezing in Jones County."

. . . Morals:

"Not a saloon in Jones County. Do you know that we consider this the grandest thing that could be said in our favor. Not a saloon in Jones County! Does not that one sentence speak volumes in favor of the morality and sobriety of our town and country?"

. . . Politics:

"In politics Jones County is Democratic, but we are not hide-bound Democrats out here. We are of the free coinage, tariff and revenue only stripe, and we don't care a Continental what ticket you vote, so you make us a peaceable, lawabiding and thrifty citizen."

. . . Negroes:

"There are but two or three negroes in Jones County, and we don't want any more. We find that we can get along better without them. This is a white man's country, and it is not degrading for a white man to work. Keep the negro out and learn your children how to work. That is the idea."

"You can grow anything in Jones County that you can grow anywhere else except negroes and tropical fruits."

The paper was boastful:

"Men who come here and see Jones County for the first time are filled with amazement. They had no idea that such a country was in existence, and they never rest until they own some of our fertile soil.''

But there was some attempt to be candid too:

''We sometimes have dust storms here that are very disagreeable, but are generally of short duration. They only serve to put a little more sand in a man's craw.''

The promoters promised rapid development:

''Anson will have a railroad within twelve months. Mark the prediction.''

The Wichita Valley rails finally were laid in 1906, fifteen years late.

For the timid, there was an appeal to courage:

''How much is the land worth that you are working to-day? $20 per acre? Well, my dear sir, you can get four acres of just as good land in Jones County for every acre of yours. Sell it and come where your children will have some opportunities. If you don't own the land you are working now, how much rent do you pay? $4 an acre? Well, sir, you deserve to be poor. Paying a good price for land every year in rent and at the end of the year poorer than when you started. Is this not slavery? Get a move on yourself. Be a man. Cut loose from old associations and your galling servitude. Come to Jones County and buy a home. Values are constantly enhancing here, and in two years the land will be worth twice as much as you paid for it. Does a sensible man want more?''

There were suggestions for new enterprises that might be expected to thrive:

> "There is a fine location here for some good man to start a dairy."
> "A good laundry would pay big money in Anson."

No appeal was spared in the effort to set the reader in motion:

> "It is common, we know, for 'boom' literature to make such claims for every county in western Texas, but reader, we ask that you come and see for yourself . . . This paper wants to see a man on every 160 acres of land in Jones County. We have the land. Now for the people."
> "Come west, young man, to make your future."

As a young man, Mart Caffey taught the one-room school near his home in the hills of Prentiss County, Mississippi. Because there was no extensive preparation required of teachers and because the pay was low, it was not at all unusual that so young a man should have this responsibility. As the teacher in the community, Mart could bring home his keep to add to what the small farm could produce and to what little compensation John Caffey might receive from his parishoners.

Among Mart's pupils was Myra Lollar, the almost-grown daughter of Giles and Sallie Lollar, who worked a farm in a hollow between the Caffey place and the Shady Grove church. She was to be Mart's wife. In the fall of 1890 it was decided that they would marry—Mart a young man of twenty-one, Myra a girl at seventeen. Mart shared his vision of a home in the new Texas country, and by the time they were wed, it was settled that their life together would take them out of Mississippi and away to the unseen prairie of Texas. There would be no tarrying in Prentiss County. One of the advantages of the move, as Mart saw it, was that it provided the convenient opportunity for leaving as much distance as possible between himself and Giles Lollar. Myra's father was a contrary and insistent sort of man, and this did not set well with Mart, who had his own stubborn streak. As it happened, this benefit was erased within a few years when Lollars migrated west by the dozens, ultimately surrounding Mart again in Jones County.

On November 11 Mart and Myra became man and wife. Within a few days they started for Texas. They didn't travel as Edgar had done, in a wagon. By now there were rail connections from Booneville down to Meridian, across Mississippi and Louisiana to the west, out of the great hardwood forests and across the prairie to Abilene, only twenty miles from the county seat of Jones County. Edgar would be in Jones County by now, would meet the train at Abilene and carry Mart and his bride to Anson. From there they would find ways to make ends meet, and to begin the pursuit of a farm home of their own.

One the day of their departure, Mart and Myra loaded their possessions on a wagon. With brothers aboard for the ride to Booneville, they rolled away from Giles Lollar's cabin. Mart didn't drive straight to town. Instead he drove the few miles over to the Bennett place to say goodbye to lifelong neighbors, and especially to his good friend Abb. From there he followed the crooks and bends of the Meadow Creek road, through the familiar hills and hollows, and beneath the bare branches of the great oaks, over the six dusty miles to the village of Booneville. When the southbound whistled and the iron wheels rolled toward Tupelo on an autumn afternoon, Mart and Myra left home and family, took each other and little else, and rode the long rail for Texas.

3. The New Country

At Meridian Mart and Myra changed trains and caught the westbound, rode across the home state and watched miles of Mississippi disappear behind them. They crossed the big river and rode past the sloughs and bayous of Louisiana. At Shreveport, the Queen and Crescent gave way to the Texas and Pacific. The T and P led on through miles of the east Texas piney woods—rolling, wooded country not so very different from northern Mississippi. The train rumbled into the cross timbers and over the level stretch to Dallas, through the city and toward the commotion of Fort Worth.

Fort Worth was "Cowtown"—a lively city of stockyards and rail sidings and the big homes of old time cattle barons who had retired or who operated their ranches from a comfortable distance. Fort Worth was also, to some extent, the jumping off place for the new country to the west, and for the distinctive region that was "West Texas." This was so partly because of geography, because Fort Worth was situated roughly in the transition zone between the eastern woods and the dry western prairie. But it was also true because of the seven years the T & P rails had spent stalled at or near Fort Worth. From 1873 to 1880 the rail builders had encountered a series of financial and legal problems that delayed completion of the line to its intended destination. For seven years, then, Fort Worth was the terminus. As such, it enjoyed the advantage of serving as the shipping point for all of West Texas. During these years, Fort Worth enjoyed a time of growth and prosperity. The town grew toward maturity in terms of city conveniences and social life as well. Thus there was something of a disparity between Fort Worth and the still-open country to the west. Even after the railroad had pushed on through West Texas, Fort Worth stayed a step ahead for many years.

The country that Mart and Myra saw when they left the stockyards and rolled west out of Fort Worth was not, strictly speaking, a frontier. It was what might better have been called a "twilight frontier," for it had neither the hazard and desolation of a true frontier nor the stable character of an area long settled and developed. Instead, West Texas was in a decade of rapid change from a wilderness to a thriving agricultural and commercial region. Throughout the new country, investors were dealing and developing, new businesses were opening, towns were growing up, new land was being cleared and broken.

From Fort Worth the rails led away due west, across the prairie and through a succession of railroad towns. Not all of the towns were new, but a good many were. In laying a route across Texas, the T & P had engaged in a game of wits that other railroad companies had discovered and refined long before. As the line was surveyed and staked, the railroad men dickered with the citizens and commercial interests of established towns that were generally in the path of the oncoming rails. The railroad was eagerly awaited in these towns, its economic advantage coveted. The rail builders took advantage of their enviable situation. If the railroad men could extract a sufficient bounty, in terms of free right of way and other concessions, the established town was favored with a place on the line. If the offer fell short of the rail company's expectations, then the company could better fatten its revenues by bypassing the older settlement and creating a new town. The railroad could then launch a promotional campaign to sell lots, and the profits of these sales were shared with the land owner. This proved to be a profitable sideline for the railroads, and the practice was instrumental in the births of numerous new towns and the demise of older ones. Towns like Fort Griffin, Belle Plain, and Buffalo Gap withered on the vine while Abilene, Baird, and Big Spring prospered.

The railroad builders had finally pushed westward

from Fort Worth in 1880. By 1882, they had reached the ultimate aim of connecting with the Pacific by meeting up with the Southern Pacific, which had its origin at San Diego. By far, most of the population and commercial activity in West Texas had come since the railroad. Except for the old frontier forts, very few settlements were as much as ten years old in 1890.

Had a traveler followed the T and P's route a few years before, he would have seen a prairie littered with massive white bones left from the slaughter of the buffalo. Across whole ranges the grasslands had been almost white with the heavy texture of the bleaching skulls, ribs, vertabrae, legs. The bones had provided a scavenger's livelihood for the first settlers. In the first years after the railroad, before the land could be made ready for production, they had picked up the bones and hauled wagonloads to the railroad to be sold for a few dollars a ton. By carloads, the buffalo bones were shipped east to be ground into fertilizer. Before many months, the prairie had been combed over.

Mart and Myra would ride as far as Abilene, the biggest of the new railroad towns. As with the other new sprung towns, Abilene could trace its beginning to a particular day in March, 1881, when town lots had been sold at auction. Before that year, there had been no dwellings at all on the site. Now, in 1890, there was a town of over three thousand people.

Abilene mirrored the in-between character of the region. It was a city in adolescence, a precarious and unstable mix of elements from the raw frontier past and from the future. Already the town had banks, churches, schools, and an opera house. The Baptists were preparing to build a college. Among the town residents were doctors, dentists, lawyers, and a young man making a living as a photographer. The town had women's clubs, lodges, and a band that came together sporadically.

At the same time, there was little about the town to indicate grace or permanence. Most of the houses and a good many of the businesses were yet of plain and hasty construction, boxed and stripped in the simplest fashion. They reflected little attention to looks, and not a great deal more to comfort. The streets were plain dirt, readily turned into a rutted bog whenever rains came. Transportation was strictly horse-drawn. Although they were uncommon, there still were public hangings occasionally. Agriculture was still in the tentative stages, much of the tillable land yet to be broken. There was still plenty of land and plenty of room for experimenting with the productive capabilities of the new soil.

When the passenger coach grated to a stop at the depot, Edgar was on the platform to meet his brother and Myra. The baggage was loaded onto Edgar's wagon, and Edgar reined the team toward Jones County and Anson. The road led north over the low hills beyond the town, then angled west toward Truby, where a bridge had been built over the Clear Fork of the Brazos.

Around Abilene and along the railroad was gentle prairie land, mainly grasslands. Away to the south was the line of low ridges that ran east and west across a few counties and made a kind of southern boundary to the country. Not many people would have called these "mountains," as some of the local people did, for they were only juniper dotted hills rising no more than perhaps two hundred feet above the prairie. About halfway across the twenty-five miles from Abilene to Anson was the beginning of the "Big Shinnery."

The shinnery lay over the prairie in a sprawling expanse. It was, in its essence, a dense thicket of native oak, shrubbery, and briars. Mesquite from the south Texas badlands was beginning to grow up among the oaks, but this was a recent development. When a man said "shinnery," he was talking about the old scrub oak thicket that the first pioneers had found. In many places the shinnery was almost impenetrable. Old timers told of how the Indians would skirt around the shinnery, never forging directly through. This knowledge had enabled the earliest settlers to build their cabins in places of refuge, tucked up against the broad side of the Big Shinnery and away from the usual paths of the Comanches. The shinnery grew over Jones County in a belt of six to ten miles wide. The dark thicket lay across the southern part of the county, roughly between the Clear Fork and Anson. It continued west into Fisher County and covered parts of Callahan, Shackelford, and Nolan as well.

To some, the low scrub shinnery might have seemed desolate and unattractive, but it did not appear so to the farmers. With some good, hard work, a man could cut the trees and grub out the stumps, so that there was tillable field. In some places there were even open or thinly wooded areas where the work was not so tedious. A man could clear as much or as little of the shinnery as he might choose. In many areas the ground was even enough that a farmer so inclined could have cleared his whole place, so that it made one broad, continuous field. In later years this was often done, but the early day farmers always left some of the shinnery standing as protected pasture for livestock and as a self renewing source of stovewood. Sometimes the pastureland was left to stand on the north, in a sort of half hopeful effort at blunting the gales that swept at the field each spring. Not much of the shinnery had been cleared in 1890, but year by year, the pioneer farmers were making headway.

Once cleared, the shinnery gave way to a dry, sandy soil that made good cotton and maize, given enough rainfall at the right time. That the needed waters would come was not a matter to be taken for granted. In that respect, West Texas was a far cry from Mississippi. The Jones County farmers didn't dig drainage ditches to carry off standing water; instead, they watched the skies daily for the prospect of vital moisture. Still, dry spells were to be expected from time to time. The farmers just prayed there wouldn't be another one like the drought of '86 and '87, when many of the new arrivals had seen two seasons of planting and hoeing come to nothing.

It wasn't long before Mart was making his way in Jones County. Shortly after his arrival, Mart helped build a school at Pleasant Hill, southwest of Anson. Mart became its first teacher. He and Myra rented a farmhouse near the school, in the same part of the county where Edgar's family lived.

After the one term of school teaching, Mart turned to the business that was his reason for being in Jones County. He wanted to farm and to have his own home and land. Lacking the money to buy, he took the path that seemed to offer the most hope to settlers of small means. He rented land and began to farm, hopeful that a few good crop years would put him in shape to buy land of his own. A percentage of each year's crop would go to the land owner, but Mart was prepared to live frugally and make the most of the margin between his rent and expenses and what he could get for the crops. It wasn't easy building up a pool of cash, not with a household to be furnished and farm equipment to be bought from scratch. Then in the fall of 1891 Olga was born, and sixteen months later another daughter, Bonnie.

*   *   *

Mart gave the enterprise a few years, but his savings weren't accumulating as fast as he had hoped. At the same time, there was talk of good homestead land available in the Indian Territory to the north. There the last of the free government lands were available to men and women strong enough to rawhide it a few seasons through the rough winters. Ever since the great land rush of 1889, other smaller parcels had periodically been taken from Indian ownership and opened to settlement.

It was also commonplace for a homesteader to find the going too rough. The land proved too much for settlers who could barely farm but who lacked the grit or ingenuity to cope with the hazards and wrestle a piece of raw land into a permanent and producing farm. Either the hardships drove them back or a few lean years put them under, so that their claims were forfeited before private ownership could be established. When a claim was forfeited, it could be filed on a second time. Where one man had failed, a stronger or luckier one might do all right. Mart thought he might be such a man. When the crop was sold and the land owner had been paid his share in the fall of '93, Mart and Myra turned back the rented land and loaded their belongings on a wagon. With winter on the way, they rolled north toward the Red River and the Indian Territory beyond.

Mart was heading for southern Oklahoma, just north a ways from Wichita Falls. By the time winter set in, he had filed on a 160 acre homestead and had bought another piece of land adjoining. On the place already were a primitive house and a shed that could be fixed up to serve well enough. Bitter gales drove at the bare board walls that first winter, but Mart and Myra and the girls stood it and were still on the land to plant when spring came round at last.

The Oklahoma territory was not quite so civilized as Jones County had been. As yet it was sparsely peopled. It was a land still not broken to orderly society, a free and open country that had its shape of rough edges and outlandish characters. As a Tulsa editor observed many years later, "When deputy marshals imposed law and order in the wild Indian Territory, there was a lot of imposing to do."

One evening while the sun settled on the western plain and dusk came over the land, Mart walked from his work in the field. As he came to the house, a horseman rode from afar, toward the house. A dark haired man rode up and spoke. Mart and the stranger talked some, and the man told of his ride and where he was going and asked whether he might feed and water his horse. The man spoke well, seemed like an all right fellow, and Mart was glad to oblige him, as was the way out in the isolated country. The man dismounted and led his horse to the barn, gave it feed and water. Supper was about to be ready, and Mart asked whether the stranger might not come on in and eat. After the meal the horseman spoke his thanks and went on his way.

Two days after the stranger's visit, two men rode up to the house, big stars gleaming on their chests. They were full of questions. Had a dark haired man passed this way? Yes. When? Two days ago. Did he say where he had come from? No. Was he jittery? Not as I could tell. Which way did he go? Well, he rode out east. Did he say where he was headed? Mart repeated the destination he had heard mentioned. The lawmen offered no information. When they were done asking questions, they rode off in a direction opposite the one Mart had indicated.

Within a few weeks came a rider delivering a summons from the federal court in Wichita Falls. Mart hadn't the money to make such a trip, and he was not much inclined to leave Myra and the girls on the isolated farmstead. He wrote the judge, asking to be excused. The judge sent money for the trip, saying, ''You be there.''

Mart traveled to Wichita Falls on the appointed day. When he walked into the courtroom, there sat the dark haired stranger. He was on trial, accused of murder and horse stealing. The trial went along and Mart was called to the witness stand. The prosecutor began his questioning, poking this way and that, trying every way possible to have Mart say something damaging to the accused man, but Mart just told plain facts as he remembered them. When the prosecutor was finished, the defense lawyer made no move to cross-examine. The judge motioned Mart's dismissal from the stand, and Mart headed for the door. As he walked past the table where the stranger was seated, the man stood to shake his hand. Mart passed on out of the courtroom and started for home.

Winters were hard on the Oklahoma plain, the summers humid and sticky. But the land was good, and Mart and Myra soon were getting ahead. They were, as folks liked to say, ''accumulatin'.'' Mart made good crops on the new soil, and over the months, he traded into a good collection of cattle and horses and hogs. You could grow chickens on the Oklahoma land without even trying; Myra's henhouse had never been so full and noisy. In the fall of 1894, another baby was born—Viola.

The land was to Mart's liking, and so was the progress he was making. The only drawback came when the little girls began to be sick all the time. When the usual remedies had been tried with no evidence of improvement, the babies were taken to the town doctor. Had he known what doctors knew later, it would have been a relatively simple matter to cure the girls; they had worms. As it was, the doctor could only tell Mart that they would never thrive in the humid country. If they were to get better, they would have to be taken to a dry climate.

When the last crop was sold and the property had been disposed of, Mart loaded the wagon and turned the mules south, urged them forward to the Red River and across into Texas, back toward Jones County. In the next years Mart rented land and farmed, saved his money and bided his time. By 1900 there were two more children, John and Sula. In 1901 Mart bought land—160 acres southwest of Anson, two miles north of the river. At six dollars an acre, it seemed like a fair deal. The family was on the place in time for spring planting, and in July, Wiley was born.

It was at about this time that Oscar Caffey picked up and made the long move from Mississippi to join his brothers in Jones County. Oscar brought a wife and five children and began farming on rented lands around Truby and the Clear Fork.

*   *   *

Life wasn't easy in the new country. The work was hard and never ending. In the beginning, the shinnery had to be cleared before there could be crops. This was backbreaking labor, hacking at the trunks of the oaks, bludgeoning at the roots with a grubbing hoe til at last the stump gave way and rolled free. Acres of loose brush had to be hauled or burned. When planting time came, Mart spent long days behind a mule, holding the steel blade of the walking buster hard into the ground to make the crop rows. In the sweltering days of summer, Mart was in the field with a hoe, chopping weeds and Johnson grass away from the young cotton plants. In fall the mature bolls had to be picked and hauled to the gin. If there was hail or drought, months of work went for little or nothing. Mart killed and dressed hogs, built fence, milked the cow, cut stovewood and hauled it from the pasture.

Myra's days were no easier. There was always a baby to care for, more often two or three. Putting meals on the table meant baking, canning, shelling peas, skinning chickens and scraping guts out of the slimy carcass. Myra stitched clothes and cotton sacks, kept the henhouse and garden.

The West Texas weather, with its spring gales and dust storms, twisters and blue northers, was fearsome to many of the settlers who had come from places where such events were unknown. Many of the farm people feared to be blown away by the violent winds that came in spring and summer, lashing the trees and sending tumbleweeds hurtling across the prairie. On most of the farmsteads, a cellar was dug near the house, a dark and narrow underground space covered with timbers and earth and approached by way of a dug out stairwell. When the northern sky turned black, mothers all across the prairie country would gather up the kids and herd them to the cellar.

Birth and death usually occurred at home, attended only by family and perhaps close neighbors. Dr. Bowyer and Dr. Stephens practiced in Anson, but many diseases were beyond their curative skills. Afflictions that later would come under control brought dread across the county whenever they cropped up among the country people. Yellow fever, tuberculosis, and pneumonia brought death into many a home on the farming frontier. Infant and child deaths were not uncommon, what with the primitive state of medicine and the hostile winter environs. A farm family had been lucky if eight or ten children could live to be grown without a loss somewhere along the line.

On the land, conveniences were non-existent. Winter and summer, in bad weather or the bitterest dark night, farm people made the trek out back to the smelly, dank outhouse for want of indoor plumbing. In southern Jones County, the ground water had a hard, bitter taste, so a deep cistern was dug beside the house to catch and store rainwater off the roof. Whenever water was needed for drinking or cooking, one of the children was sent to toss the bucket into the deep shaft and draw it up full of water. Ever so often a cup of coal oil was dumped into the cistern to kill the bugs. The kerosene formed a film on top of the water and gave it a bad taste. Periodically one of the boys was lowered into the cistern to clean out the trash and scum. Walls were hollow and the house drafty, the winter chill only dulled by low heat from an iron stove or fireplace. In summer, a person could sweat through the night inside the house or take his chances with the mosquitoes on the porch. Whenever it was time to plow or plant or drive to town, a team of mules or horses had first to be found in the back of the pasture and driven up to the barn to be harnessed and hitched.

People did for themselves. When an infant was born, the cord might be tied and the whole affair managed by a husband or neighbor woman. When someone died, the body was dressed for burial by the same people who had loved the departed one in life and cared for him in sickness. Whatever food appeared on the table at mealtimes was the result of normal farmstead chores. If there was milk, it had come from one of the boys pulling on the teats of a milk cow in the early hours. If there was pork, it was there only because a hog had been fattened through the fall, then knocked in the head with an axe, scalded in a barrel, cleaned and dressed in early winter.

Frontier life was more severe than many of the settlers

had supposed it would be. Prosperity was elusive, mere survival a struggle. The faith that had come from the old country now gave solace in days of hardship, raised hopes for final victory after the toilsome days on earth. At brush arbor meetings in summer and at the more frequent preaching days at the schoolhouse, the people sang of earthly cares and heavenly promises. From the homes back south had come copies of the *Old Harp Song Book,* the ones that opened out longways, thick with pages of the old, mildly dissonant hymns. The odd looking shape notes traced doleful tunes, most of them pitched in a minor key. They were songs of strife and hope:

. . . A home in Heaven! What a joyful thought,
     As the poor man toils his weary lot:
     His heart oppressed and with anguish driv'n
     From his home on earth to his home in Heaven . . .

. . . A few more days, or years at most,
     My troubles will be o'er;
     I hope to join the heav'nly host
     On Canaan's happy shore . . .

. . . On Jordan's stormy banks I stand
     And cast a wishful eye,
     To Canaan's fair and happy land
     Where my possessions lie . . .

. . . While trav'ling through this veil of tears,
     Amidst temptations, doubts and fears,
     Our saviour by his precious grace,
     Has offer'd us a home—a better place . . .

. . . When I can read my title clear
     To mansions in the skies,
     I'll bid farewell to ev'ry fear
     And dry my weeping eyes . . .

Similar beliefs were expressed in the inscriptions carved on the plain marble slabs planted over the graves of the early settlers at Mount Hope and the smaller rural churchyard cemeteries over Jones County:

"Resting in hope of a glorious resurrection."

"No pain, no grief, no anxious fear,
Can reach the peaceful sleeper here."

"Too good for earth, God called them home."

A special kind of grief came when a child was suddenly taken. But many of the early families, at one time or another, had to see a little one placed in the ground under the small mound that told its own story. Still, they looked to faith in a better hereafter for comfort:

"Happy infant early blest,
Rest in peace, in slumber rest."

"From mother's arms to the arms of Jesus."

The burdens of life in the new country could be better endured in the faith that, no matter how despairing present times might be, to all who believed would come a great reward in a land beyond the grave.

*   *   *

Mart was ever on the lookout for a way to improve his situation. There were six kids already and sure to be more, so Mart felt a certain urgency for getting ahead a little more each year. When, in 1904, Mart had the chance to trade for a better farmstead, he took it. The place Mart wanted was a few miles to the south and east, a quarter section with a good house, a half mile from the newly built Elliott school. In cultivation was the one continuous broad field of good sandy land. The field covered sixty or more acres, all cleared and well drained, protected on the north and west by shinnery pasture.

In order to have the place, Mart did what, for him, was a very unusual thing. He put up a thousand dollars cash and accepted the discomfort of being in debt for another thousand. Mart signed a note calling for payments of $250 on the first day of January each year—1905, 1906, 1907, 1908. What was more typical of Mart was that the note came to be paid off in full by the spring of 1905, so that Mart held clear title and owed no one. Mart moved the family and sold the other land. He wouldn't move again. Instead, the next years were to be spent in improving the place into a productive farm and a good home.

News traveled from the far home country to find Mart in midsummer, 1906. Nancy, his mother, was sick and dying in the old hills near Booneville. John was long since dead—he had gone during Mart's time in the Indian Territory. For twelve years it had been just the young brother Fletcher, his wife Mary, and Nancy living on the old Mississippi home. Mart went to Oscar and Edgar, talked the situation through, decided to make the journey back to Mississippi to see his mother while she lived. Edgar would go too. Mart and Edgar lit out for Abilene to catch the eastbound train.

Yellow fever was raging in east Texas, and after Fort Worth the going was slow. There were long delays and unexplained stops—frustrating times when Mart and Edgar fidgeted anxious and ignorant while train men and town men stood huddled on the platform. A journey that should have taken three days wore on for a week. Where towns had been quarantined with the worsening of the epidemic, travelers entering town by any means were held and not permitted to leave, rail passengers included. To keep from being waylaid, Mart and Edgar jumped the train a ways out of town, walked out around the streets and houses, boarded again when the train rolled out into open country on the far side.

By the time Mart and Edgar reached the northern hills and found their way to the home cabin, their mother was dead and buried in the old churchyard at Shady Grove. Mart and Edgar stayed a few days in the familiar hills, talked to the younger brother about the Texas country, urged him to come along back to Jones County with them, to leave the old times behind now. Fletcher was now thirty-two, married, still making scruffy crops on the overworked patch that had been about worn out when John bought it twenty years before. Fletcher was not keen for new horizons, but in the end he sold out and took the train west with Mart and Edgar. By early fall, Fletcher had his own small piece of the Jones County shinnery, two miles east of Mart and a half mile back from the road.

By the end of 1906, there was nothing left of the old preacher's family in Mississippi. Instead, the four sons were wintering on scattered farm places in the shinnery land of Jones County. When the bleak Texas prairie saw traces of springtime, they would break the crusty soil and plant cotton.

4. Uncle Edgar

From the time he came to Texas until his death in 1911, Edgar Caffey never stayed put anywhere more than a few years. After leaving Mississippi in 1878 at the age of twenty-two, Edgar was destined to move again and again during the rest of his fifty-five years.

When Edgar and Piney rolled away from Booneville and pointed their wagon toward Texas, the baby Sam rode with them. An earlier child had died, but there would be plenty more, twelve in all. Edgar's wagon joined several others, and together they were ferried across the churning Mississippi to begin the trek down across Arkansas and a corner of Oklahoma, over the Red River and into nothern Texas.

Edgar and Piney stopped in Wise County, near Decatur, north of Fort Worth and not far from the Indian Territory. Edgar went to farming—that was what he had come for—but it took only a few months for him to know that he would never thrive happily on a life of frontier farming. Edgar wasn't the settling kind, nor was he the type to fix his mind on a task that called for steady work, or to bind himself to a solitary routine dictated by the changing seasons. Edgar hadn't the patience to tie himself to a piece of new ground and grub out the brush, fence the land, and commit his earnings to a mortgage and his fortunes to the mercy of the Texas weather.

Fort Worth was bristling with the noisy commerce of stockyards and shipping pens and railway traffic. With the new freight lines now shipping cattle east directly from Texas, transactions once carried on at the northern railheads now took place in Fort Worth. And with the long trail drives no longer needed, big outfits could no longer

40

monopolize the cattle industry. There was more room now for the small-time stockman—the itinerant trader and the farmer who pastured cattle as a sideline. Fort Worth was infected with cowboys and ranchmen and cattle buyers, and Edgar easily caught the trading bug. He enjoyed the buying and selling, dealing and dickering, seeing his investment go good or bad in a relatively short span of time. Moreover, Edgar enjoyed the social aspects of stock trading. He like being around the storytellers, tobacco spitters, and good-time whiskey drinkers who inevitably turned up where there was trading to be done. It beat walking behind a plow.

Though his heart was not in it, Edgar had to farm a little all along, for the cattle trade could not alone support a family that continued to grow steadily. Early in his Texas years, then, Edgar fell into a pattern that he would follow all his days—one of renting and farming and trading and moving, of living always for the present and not for some vague reward that would have to be delayed through years of joyless work and sacrifice.

By 1890, Edgar knew of Jones County. With the eastern and middle counties now about saturated with farmers, it was the western counties that were offering land bargains and opportunities for new businesses. With Mart ready to make a move west, it seemed a good time for Edgar to make a change too. He and Piney sold out in Wise County, packed up their belongings and seven children, and pointed the team south and west toward wider spaces. By fall the family was settled and Edgar could meet his younger brother and Myra at the depot in Abilene, help them find a place to live and steer them toward leads on a livelihood for the first months.

Texas was a big place for a man chasing opportunity. To be sure that one had chosen the right place to invest his years was not so easy a matter so, like many others, Edgar and Mart spent some early, restless years following the rumors of better pickings. In the winter of 1893-94 Mart and Myra sold out in Jones County and went to see about the Indian Territory and Edgar took his family back north. In the wagon they went, Edgar and Piney and eight children—back toward the Red River and into the coming winter. As they rode, Piney was heavy with their ninth child.

Part way across Haskell County, the baby would be quiet inside Piney no more. Edgar stopped at a lonesome ranch house and found a welcome. For hours they struggled, Piney agonizing and the baby trying to be born. Edgar coped on through it as best he could and worried himself into a state of despair and frustration. At last he laid his head in his hands and gave up. Edgar asked one of the ranch hands whether he might ride for the doctor, some fifteen miles away. While daylight passed and the night set in, Edgar waited. When the doctor finally came and the baby had been brought safely into the world, Edgar called him Haskell. It wasn't the worst that could have happened to the boy; they might easily have been a few miles to the east in Throckmorton County. As it was, the family got itself back together and moved on northward and into the flurries of early snow. When the snow lasted into a winter storm, Piney and the child were left at Seymour to be brought along later. Edgar and the rest went on to the new home near Bowie, in Montague County.

In two years time Edgar had changed his mind yet again, had decided that the Jones County land was really more promising after all. For the last time, he took Piney and all the kids and made the long haul down across pieces of a half dozen counties. Edgar settled southwest of Anson and spent the next fifteen years renting and farming and handling cattle—a year here, a year or two there. In the first years the family lived just out of Anson on the little road that ran to Truby and Abilene, out in the open country where the wild burros still ran loose to be caught and ridden by the town boys and by Edgar's own kids.

Edgar's children could count on a move almost every year, sometimes only a stone's throw to a different house, sometimes as much as ten or twelve miles. With the moves coming after crops were in each fall, the already short school term was further disrupted. At best the country schools might be open for only five or six months of the year, and when the boys were needed in the field at picking time, more days were lost. Altogether, circumstances didn't allow for much in the way of schooling. Eight or nine years of sporadic attendance left one of Edgar's children with maybe all of fifteen months spent in studies. Whatever else Edgar may have left with his children, an education was not part of the legacy.

There was much about Edgar to reflect his concern with the immediate and his lack of interest in the long term. This was especially true in contrast to the more disciplined ways of his brother Mart. Mart practiced thrift, and preached it as well. "A penny saved is a penny made," he would say. Mart was loath to go into debt for any reason, preferring to stick close on his spending if need be. A guest at Mart's table could be assured of plenty to eat, but not of a full set of utensils. Mart saw no need to have the extras on hand just for the occasional times when there might be company to serve. Edgar was more the free spender. He had no fear of indebtedness, lived on credit from year to year as naturally as Mart avoided it. Edgar's credit was good, at least until the last years. Up until then, he could send one of the kids to any store in Anson knowing that his name would be a sufficient guarantee for the purchase. Debts accumulated through the spring and summer, but as soon as crops were sold in the fall, they were all paid off.

Edgar had a taste for whiskey, more than a social one, in fact. This came to be one of the characteristics by which he was known and remembered. Edgar's drinking made steady demands on the family purse and neutralized his otherwise capable productive faculties. Edgar was no down and out drunkard, but his attraction to the bottle took time from other labors and distracted him from more constructive aims, until it was plain that his accomplishments were less than they might easily have been otherwise. Too much of Edgar went to waste in deadened evenings at the house and long afternoons in town. The example was not lost on Edgar's family. Mart saw the ruinous effects on his brother and refused to allow any kind of alcohol in his own house. When Haskell grew up enough to read the Bible's pronouncement on liquor, he knew too well what it meant: "Wine is a mocker and strong drink a brawler, and whosoever is deceived thereby is not wise."

Whatever his imperfections, Edgar was well regarded by his neighbors, loved and admired by his family. Edgar did have a way with people—a genuine liking for them that made it possible to overlook his flaws and appreciate his easy warmth. Edgar, with his gregarious ways, soon knew most everyone around the south part of Jones County. His house became a welcome stop for neighbors, an early stopping place for a man considering a run at one of the county offices.

Like his brothers, Edgar had been brought up by his father to read and respect the Bible, and he taught his own growing children to read and study its words too. Just as Haskell would live to quote the scriptures in condemnation of alcohol, Luther, in his grown years, could turn to Bible verses that he offered as proof that the Bible commended strong drink to its readers in some circumstances. Piney's favorite time of day was the early morning. In the peaceful early hours, she and Edgar rose and left the children sleeping. Piney fired the stove and set about cooking breakfast while Edgar sat at the kitchen table and read the Bible aloud.

As a boy Edgar studied and memorized scriptures. When the Sunday school contests were held, he recited alongside the other young ones and on one occasion won the silver cup that went to the pupil who had learned the lessons best of all. Edgar prized that cup; it came with him to Texas and occupied a place of honor in each different house, well up into his middle years. After one of the later moves, the cup came to rest on a shelf above the kitchen stove. There it remained until a day when one of the family went rummaging for some hidden item on the shelf. The cup was set down on the stove for the moment, then forgotten. When Haskell came into the kitchen, the cup had melted into a puddle that ran in bright rivulets and filled the eyes of the old iron stove. Haskell was heartsick at the sight. He killed the fire and agonized over the carelessness of the irretrievable moment just past. When the stove was cool, Haskell picked up the mottled bits of silver and put them in a cigar box.

Edgar was never destined for a long life. He hadn't the qualities of which old age is fashioned. Edgar was prone to respiratory troubles—twice had survived pneumonia, twice refused to be bothered with precautions. Neither did his drinking ways proffer a pleasant journey into old age. Year upon year, it took something more out of him. If Edgar had ever planned to be old, there was nothing to show it. He went on living a year at a time, never sliding into disgrace and ruin, never accumulating the durable properties and sensible habits that might have sustained him later.

Edgar's end began with an act of kindness. The grown daughter Myrtle, at home across the county with her farmer husband, had lost a baby in childbirth. When Edgar heard, he went to her, stayed with her, did his best to offer comfort. When night fell over the house, he lay down to sleep on the floor by the stove, a quilt drawn up around him against the draft. It was here that Edgar took pneumonia for the third time.

Edgar was taken home to his own house, put to bed in the front room. Piney cared for him just as she had done before, but Edgar went downhill. When he took a turn for the worse, the grown sons and brothers came. Early of an evening Edgar called Tom and Sam to the bed and asked that they stand him up. The boys put Edgar on his feet and he smoothed his own bedclothes, lest the lights go out for him and leave him a rumpled sight before them all. Toward bedtime Mart took the younger ones in hand. "There's nothing more you boys can do," he told them, "You might as well go on to bed."

Sometime near midnight Mart came tumbling into the bedroom and woke the sleepers. "Boys, you'd better get out there—your Pa's just about gone." The grown ones were still in the front room gathered round Edgar's bed, watching while he slipped away. Haskell went to the bedside and felt his father's arm, put his cheek on Edgar's. The life was gone out of him. Haskell walked back through the kitchen, out into the yard and back away from the house, and cried.

Edgar was buried in Mount Hope Cemetery, on a gentle rise just out of Anson toward Albany and the east. Over his grave was stood the six foot high monument made to mark the resting place of one of Edgar's lodge, the Woodmen of the World. It was a massive granite tree trunk with nubs of branches all around, bark-like grooves textured into the stone, and the circular fraternal seal set into the stone. When Edgar's death had appeared to him more than an even bet, he had instructed Tom regarding the two thousand dollars in insurance money that would be coming in through the lodge. Fourteen hundred dollars would be put toward his debts; that would pay them off in full. The rest was for Piney.

Haskell was seventeen years old when Edgar's death left him with his mother and the three younger girls to look after. Tom and Sam and "T" had their own land to work now, their own families to provide for. It was all any of them could manage to make do for their own. It was for Haskell to worry about what was left of the family at home, Piney and the little ones—Lula Mae and Allie and Bessie.

After Edgar was gone the family quit moving around and stayed on at the place where he had died. "We battled it out," Haskell recalled, "rentin' and farmin'." In ten years time Haskell had made ten crops on the place, had managed to pay it out and own it.

By 1920 the girls were grown and out on their own. Piney moved in to Anson to live with Lula Mae in a house that Haskell had bought. Haskell stayed on the Jones County land twenty-seven more years before moving west to new country in Howard County. He would live to farm thirteen years there and twenty more in Martin County, working well up into his eighties. Haskell carried with him always a hatred of whiskey, a love of the Bible, and an eye for good cattle.

5. The Home Place

Mart Caffey's family moved to the home place in 1904 and kept it for nearly sixty years—for as long as Mart or Myra lived, and a few years more. For a good many years, up until the changes triggered by the Depression, the home place was part of an era that flourished and then passed—an era when large families lived on small farms, when country schools and churches were scattered over the rural countryside, when rural areas were alive with children and horses and mules and hogs and chickens and the varied lives of people doing for themselves. It was a time when the mainstream—a slower moving mainstream—ran as much through the country places as through cities and towns. Most of the people in Jones County lived and worked on the farms, with the towns mainly serving as sources of supply and service to the basic enterprise of agriculture. The farms were, by and large, peopled by men and women of faith and ambition—people who wanted to get ahead and to see their children prosper and succeed. During these years the country people enjoyed the new inventions and conveniences along with the city people. Telephones, autos, and phonographs became commonplace along the country lanes, with only a short lag behind the latest style in Anson.

As long as cotton was high and farming technology was low, the pattern held. Though prices might vary from year to year, a farmer could generally expect to have a good income and provide reasonably well for a family. Eventually the economic structure of the small farms would crumble and disintegrate, times would change and a way of life would cease to be. Mart's children thus grew up in a world that vanished behind them like morning fog from a

Mississippi hollow. The childhood they remembered would come to seem quaint and antiquated to their own children and leave them to muse on their childhood experiences and conclude, "Them days are gone forever."

The home place was five miles south of Anson, out in the country and away from any main road. To the east was the new road to Abilene and over west was the old road through Truby. In between were the quiet miles of shinnerylands crisscrossed with dirt lanes and dotted with farmhouses. The land was almost level, gentle slopes rising and falling gradually and almost imperceptibly over the broad stretches. The countryside was a patchwork of farms, each of eighty to one hundred and sixty acres. Sandy fields were cleared from out of the shinnery in varied squares and rectangles, tracts of wooded land left standing next to them.

The early developers of the Jones County farm lands divided and subdivided, surveyed and sold off the various farm tracts. The land was divided into "sections," each one a mile square and containing 640 acres. The section was split into farms of 80 or 160 acres, with odd sizes coming about as one man might sell part of his land to a neighbor. The home place took up the southeast quarter of a section of land in the Elliott community. Dirt roads ran the length of each side of the larger section, so that there was road all around its perimeter and along the south and east sides of Mart's quarter section. To the west was Oliver Thompson's field and to the north, Dixon's field and pasture. On the far corner was the Spurling place.

The home place was part of what had once been "the Big Shinnery." By the time Mart bought the place, a good many settlers had moved in, cleared fields, and established farms, so that there were now broad, open expanses among the remaining stands of woodlands. On Mart's own farm the clearing had begun on the south end, where the soil was sandy and the trees sparse and more easily uprooted. The field covered perhaps sixty acres, stretching from the house and lot on the west to the boundary lane a half mile

49

east. Behind the field to the north was the heavy bank of shinnery pasture. Over the years, Mart cleared out more of the shinnery, adding acreage to the field and pushing the line of trees back farther north. A few acres at a time, the trees were grubbed out and cleared off, first by Mart himself and later by itinerant laborers. Finally the field came to cover perhaps a hundred acres or more.

When Mart bought the home place, a good enough house already stood on the high ground by the west fenceline, facing out on the road. Behind the house was the chicken coop, then the lot and barn, and a narrow strip of pasture that ran back north along the fenceline to connect with the greater part of the pasture in the back. Directly across the road was the Elliott place, the farmhouse off the road and back down a narrow lane. East a half mile along the road and just over on Elliott's near corner was the one-room Elliott Schoolhouse.

When Mart's family moved to the home place in 1904, there were already seven children, four girls and three boys. Olga was now twelve years old, the others stairstepping downward in age, each a year or two apart, on down to the new baby boy, Rudolph. This was pretty much of the way among the farm families. The large family provided more hands for the field work, and to some, more children symbolized the productive citizen as well. Over the next ten years, Myra continued to be pregnant or tending a new baby most of the time. In all, four more boys were born. Preston, born in 1906, lived only sixteen months and died of intestinal problems. He was buried in the hilltop cemetery at Truby, five miles to the south and west. Boyd, Dalton, and Glenn all thrived and grew to put in many long days chopping cotton and hauling wood on the way to other pursuits.

For almost twenty years, into the mid-1920s, the home place rocked along in its prime—plenty of children to keep the household noisy and interesting, plenty of work to be kept up in the field and pasture, new developments and inventions coming along every few years. These were years of school days and courting times, of circus trips and endless capers and adventures. Throughout the early years, the family was made up of the four older girls, the string of younger brothers, and John, who didn't fit very neatly into either group.

Beyond the fences of the home place was a world of interesting people and places. It stretched north to Anson, east to the Abilene road, west to Truby, and south to the Clear Fork. It included all that Mart's younger boys might have required for a full and lively youth. The prairie rolled away in all directions from the farmhouse on the road, and Mart's boys followed, over the miles of woods and fields and along the dirt lanes that led away to various kinds of fun and adventure.

A good half hour's walk to the south was the Clear Fork of the Brazos—slow moving, still, and contrary to its name, generally muddy. Willows swayed their gentle, fluid motions along the banks and great elms spread wide to shade the river. Mart's boys approached the Clear Fork by a road that snaked southward from Oliver Thompson's corner, or by way of a shortcut across Elliott's field and the farms beyond. The objective usually was "Phone Crossing," a shallow ford where the earliest Anson to Abilene road had once crossed before the bridge was built farther west at Truby. When phone lines came to the Elliott community just before the first world war, the line followed the older route, so that the ford came to be known as "Phone Crossing." Near the crossing was a deeper hole where the farm kids went swimming, and all along the channel were bluecats that could generally be counted on to bite on minnows or worms. On overnight outings the boys would sometimes seine for minnows, then set a line across the river. By morning they could often pull the heavy line out of the water to find spiny, snubnosed catfish squirming all along it. Phone Crossing was where families spent leisurely Sunday afternoons and it was where the schoolboys frolicked when they played hookey on April Fool's Day. It was also the scene of occasional baptisms performed by the Holiness preacher, who made a great to-do whenever another converted sinner went under.

Away to the north of the home place, some six miles distant, was the town of Anson. At the very center of Anson was the elaborate, silver domed courthouse, visible from afar in any direction. Around the courthouse, shops and businesses were arranged in a town square, a place where country people milled and shopped and visited in droves most every Saturday. Around 1910 a moving picture house went into business, and it quickly became a focus of keen interest for the country boys who marveled at the escapades of Tom Mix and Hopalong Cassidy. On the north side of the square was the opera house, built in 1907, in a shortlived era when a good many West Texas towns were giving high culture a fling. Anson was the source of lumber and feed, harness and seed and farm implements; food staples and store bought britches. On trading days, when the country men swarmed in with cattle and horses and mules and what-have-you, it was the scene of considerable headscratching and of quite a few hasty decisions—some good, some not so good.

To the east of the farm were two places of particular interest. Just up the road and across to the east from the home place was Bob White's farm, and of more immediate importance, Bob White's peach orchard and watermelon patch. Mart Caffey's boys were subscribers to the notion that stolen fruit tastes best, so they occasionally made night visits to the White place during the summer growing season to make off with a watermelon under one arm or with a hatful of plump, tree ripened peaches. Part of the fun of these sortees was, of course, the adventure of sneaking up to capture the goods at the risk of being caught. On one occasion Drayte Hawthorne accompanied the Caffey boys and dared to snatch a bowl of fresh sliced peaches off the kitchen windowsill. When Mrs. White walked into the kitchen at the critical moment, Drayte found it necessary to quit the premises in a hurry. He took off with the bowl and alledgedly jumped the fence without spilling a drop of the juice.

Another mile up the road to the east, then back south in the shinnery, was the backwoods farm where Uncle Fletcher and Aunt Mary lived. Mary's cooking and Fletcher's interesting way of talking made this a favorite visiting place for Fletcher's many nieces and nephews.

*   *   *

All around the home place were neighbor families. These provided playmates for the younger children and courting partners for the older ones. Among the adults there were some colorful personalities—interesting characters to know and remember. Most of these people had come to the new country by the same general path as Mart and Myra—leaving poor lives in the older southern states to seek better times in an unseen land to the west. The Hawthornes and the Shirleys were from Alabama, the Rices and the Smiths from Georgia. Several families of Lollars had followed Mart and Myra from Mississippi, Myra's parents included. Other neighbors had come from Arkansas, Tennessee, or the Carolinas.

There were six boys and two girls in the Elliott family across the road. The boys were slightly older, on the whole, than Mart's bunch of boys. Ben, the youngest, was the same age as Wiley, and the two became fast friends for life. A year or two older was Guy. In the middle were twin boys who could hardly have been less alike. Where Charlie was affable and soft spoken and civil, George was brash and talkative—sometimes outgoing and gregarious in a pleasant way, sometimes rowdy and belligerent. George was a fighting sort of fellow, and he went around kicking up minor scrapes all over the Elliott community in his younger days. Finally he went off to the Navy and came back a few years later, all full of sass and confidence, only to run head on into Carl Lollar, who had grown into quite a man in his absence. When Carl Lollar had finished with George, George had lost all interest in fighting and was ready to settle down and make a farmer and a good neighbor.

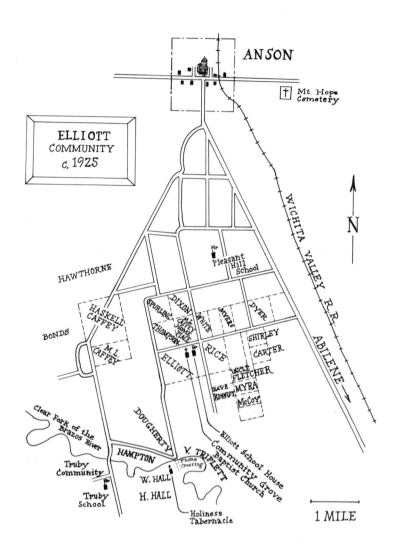

ANSON

Mt. Hope Cemetery

ELLIOTT
COMMUNITY
c. 1925

N

WICHITA VALLEY R.R. — ABILENE

HAWTHORNE

Pleasant Hill School

HASKELL CAFFEY

BONDS

M.L. CAFFEY

SPURLING
DIXON
WHITE
M.L. CAFFEY HOME PLACE
THOMPSON

MYERS

DYER

SHIRLEY

CARTER

RICE

UNCLE FLETCHER

ELLIOTT

DAVE KENNEDY

MYRA

McCOY

Clear Fork of the Brazos River

DOUGHERTY

Elliott School House
Community Grove Baptist Church

HAMPTON

V. TRIPLETT

Phone Crossing

Truby Community

W. HALL

Truby School

H. HALL

Holiness Tabernacle

1 MILE

Older still were Mendel and Gray Elliott. Mendel was something of a curiosity, a pious and self-important sort of fellow who often amused the neighbor boys when he fully intended to be acting in a serious manner. Mendel had gone off to the Appalachian country to serve as a missionary. Some years later he visited back home and neighbors asked what he had been up to. Mendel's reply was rapid and concise, rattled out in his sharp edged, high pitched voice: "Teaching and preaching, teaching and preaching." On one visit home Mendel accompanied his younger brother Charlie to Anson on some errand, and in the course of things, Charlie happened to conclude a very excellent trade. When the two men shared a bed that night, Charlie snoozed off as usual, but Mendel was wakeful and restless. Finally he shook his brother awake and spoke up: "Cholly—Cholly, are you sure you didn't cheat that fella?"

On a corner across from the home place was the John Rice place. John had to make do with a smaller family than most, three boys and two girls. Menco Rice, the oldest, was Wiley's age, and then came two sisters who made poor company for Menco's boyhood interests. Menco thus found his companionship among the Caffey boys, and he spent as much time with them as he could. One of Menco's regular habits was to play off sick in his father's field and be sent to the house, only to turn up in Mart Caffey's field working with Wiley and Rudolph and chopping more cotton than anyone else there.

Menco once took a special liking to a calf that his father was feeding out. Menco trained the calf for riding, put a bridle over his head and rode him all over the Elliott country. When Menco went to the supper table one evening to find that the calf's time had come and that his pet calf was now on the platter before him as roast beef, he lost all interest in eating, left the table and went off to bed without supper.

Dolly White was the self-appointed respository of information about all kinds of goings on in the Elliott community. She knew all about the newest babies, about the latest developments in each courtship, about any recent whisper of scandal. She knew just about everything that went on or that was supposed to have gone on in the community. Dolly got most of her information via the party line telephone that the White family shared with neighbor farm families. More than anyone else, Dolly got her money's worth from the phone. As soon as breakfast was over, Dolly was one the phone, and she didn't put it down until time to go and make dinner for Bob and the kids. Then she talked all afternoon until suppertime. One morning one of the neighbors found the annoyance too much to bear any longer. Impatient to make her own phone call, she broke in to tell Dolly, "Mrs. White, did you know your hen house is on fire?" Dolly put up the receiver and ran horrified to find her hen house standing as usual while the neighbor went ahead to make her call.

On the south bank of the Clear Fork, just across the river below Phone Crossing, was the Hall place. That was where Henry Hall lived, along with his wife, his son Willie, and his prized wolf hounds. Henry's sport was to loose the hounds of an evening and follow them over the countryside chasing coyotes. All night long neighbors in their beds would hear the distant yelping and baying of the hounds on the chase, now to the south near the river, now to the west, now over north toward Pleasant Hill. Henry and Willie would follow the hounds ahorseback all through the night, calling them in at daybreak with a horn. When the sun came up Henry took the dogs home, but he didn't go to bed. Instead he went to work and did a full day's farm work as usual.

The Elliott community had its few ne'er do well characters. One of these men was Myra's brother-in-law, the no good husband of her sister Daisy. Daisy's husband was as shiftless as she was kind and patient, and he brought the family untold misery and embarrassment in the years before he ran off for good. He was a blustery windbag of a man, one who tried to get what he wanted by bluff instead of by work. He won the enmity of the neighbors and the scorn and disgust of men like Mart. Finally, he took as much of the family property as he could get his hands on and went off to live in a hotel on the south side of Abilene.

*   *   *

The home place had its own personality—its own face, its wrinkles and its idiosyncrasies. Like the farms around it, it had been hewn out of the country by hand, so that its features were distinctive and unique and inimitable. The house, the barn, the pasture, the cellar and the cistern and the slough in the corner of the field—these were like no other anywhere. The intimacy with which the growing children came to know all of these things finally made them "home."

The old house served for twenty years before Mart would tear it down and build a new one. The house was "L" shaped, with a covered porch and scroll trim along the front and a breezeway between the two main sections. Mart and Myra occupied the big front room, with the girls across the open breezeway and the dining room and kitchen behind. A fireplace and a wood stove provided uneven pockets of warmth in the winter months. The boys' room was at the very back, at the end of the long row of rooms running back north from the main front room. With the birth of two or three new children, Mart added another room onto the back of the original house.

The old house was built on posts, on a foundation of the kind known as "post and pier." That is, several massive posts were sunken into the ground and sawed off level and a platform floor was built on them with no underpinnings involved. This configuration left an open space between the floor and the ground, so that a person might stand out east of the house and see the sun setting underneath it in the west, which Glen often did as a small boy.

57

This kind of construction had its advantages and disadvantages. On the one hand, it left a shaded and easily accessible space where certain food supplies might be kept cool on occasion. It also provided handy storage for ladders, cane poles, and other odd items. And it did away with the likelihood that a skunk or possum would take up nesting under the house, as it might do with an enclosed foundation. There were disadvantages too, as the neighbors learned one afternoon when a rattlesnake got under Bob White's house.

Dolly White was an excitable sort of woman, easily flustered by problems that might have been of small consequence to others. With Bob gone to town for the day and a rattler underneath the house, she was beside herself, afraid to set foot outside the door and unable to go on about her business until the crisis was resolved.

Dolly got on the party line and began phoning neighbors, intent on securing help in rousting the snake. The calls produced no volunteers, but within a couple of hours, everyone in this part of the county knew about the rattlesnake under Bob White's house.

It happened that Roy Shirley, a boy of fourteen or fifteen, came walking up the road, ambling in the general direction of home. Mrs. White called out from the screen door, anxious that Roy stop and render aid in her distress. Roy listened while she spilled out the story.

''Do you have a shotgun?'' he asked, somewhat interested by now.

''Yes, we have a shotgun.''

''Have you got any loads for it?''

''Well, yes, I think so.''

Bob White's wife got the shotgun and shells, and Roy loaded the gun, closed the breech, and crouched at the side of the house. Sure enough, there was the rattlesnake, right there under the house. Roy put the gun butt to his shoulder and cut loose, blasting the rattlesnake to smithereens.

Only trouble was, the shattering shotgun blast went

in under the house, through the space underneath, out the other side, and killed four chickens scratching in the yard. The next house that Bob White built had a foundation that went all the way to the ground.

Mart's family never had quite this sort of trouble with their own house on posts, but it was a nuisance in other ways. Hens often tried to protect their eggs from being gathered and cooked over easy by laying them up under the house. When this happened, one of the smaller boys would have to be sent scrooching in under the floor on hands and knees to retrieve them. When Mart had put up with this arrangement long enough, he bought a roll of chicken wire in town and went all around the foundation nailing the wire mesh over the open space.

To the west side of the house was the cellar, a door sticking up above ground level to cover the dark passageway down the steps to the underground room. Just north of the cellar stood the outhouse, a one-holer.

Out back was the chicken coop and the bare yard where the chickens hobbled around scratching for feed. The chickens were part of Myra's domain, and she fed them and gathered the eggs. Mart and Myra followed a time honored division of labor and property commonly subscribed to by the farm couples. Myra did the gardening and took care of the chickens, and kept for her personal, unrestricted use the money made from the sale of eggs and butter.

Behind the hen house, just in the edge of the pasture, was the lot and barn. Here the feed and equipment were stored and the livestock was fed and tended. Off the barn was a pen where hogs were kept for the family's use. At harvest time, Mart filled the barn with maize, some of which would be sold to neighbors who invariably failed to plant enough to last them through the winter.

One corner of the barn was reserved for corn, which Mart kept and fed to the hogs in the weeks just before they would be slaughtered. Hog killing time came in the late fall, just before the first real cold spell. When Mart rose on

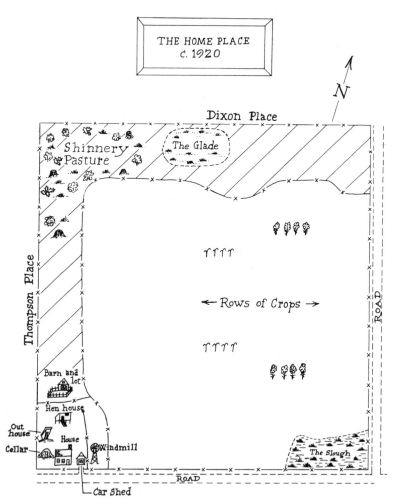

THE HOME PLACE
c. 1920

N

Dixon Place

Shinnery Pasture

The Glade

Thompson Place

ROAD

← Rows of Crops →

Barn and lot

Hen house

Out house

Cellar

House

Windmill

The Slough

Car Shed

ROAD

Corner to Corner = 1/2 Mile

a November morning and sauntered outside to find a new chill in the air, he was apt to walk back in the house and announce, "I believe I'll kill a hog." After breakfast he took the boys and went to the barn to butcher the first of three or four hogs. After knocking the animal in the head with an ax, Mart and the boys would cut the jugular vein and string the animal up by its hind legs to bleed out. Then the carcass was scalded in a barrel so that the hair could be cleaned off. The hog was gutted and butchered, and finally salted, so that the meat could be preserved.

The pasture extended back and around through the northwest corner of the property and on around to the eastern boundary. During the grass season the pasture held as many cows as it would support. Horses and mules grazed and wandered among the trees and shrubs the year round. For many years these animals were essential to the farm life. They pulled the plow and planter, hauled heavy loads in the wagon, provided transportation when saddled and ridden or hitched to a buggy.

There were perhaps twenty or thirty or more mules and horses on the home place over the years, with four or five around at any one time. There were workhorses like Jud and Ball and Shorty. Some of the animals had colorful personalities or characteristics that made them memorable—Old Beck, a cantankerous mule who didn't like anyone getting around his head, a horse called Flag because of the shape of the brand on his rump. Others passed through without leaving much of an impression. But the horse remembered most of all was Old Brigham—hands down, no contest.

Old Brigham was a big sorrel horse. He came to the home place around 1910 and was part of it for nearly fifteen years. Brigham was there during the prime years of crops, fishing trips, courting experiences, and Saturday jaunts to Anson. Several of the Caffey children grew from childhood to leaving time during the years that Brigham roamed Mart Caffey's pasture.

Whenever any family member later recalled an incident involving a horse, the one mentioned almost always was Old Brigham. Whatever they were up to, Old Brigham was there. Brigham was rough to ride, but this never kept one of the boys from a journey to town and the picture show; if he had a bucket of eggs for his way in, off he rode. Mart rode Old Brigham when he drove calves over to Tom Caffey's place. Hitched up to a buggy, Brigham took Olga to school the year she taught at Hollis Hill, several miles to the east. Brigham carried Viola all over the south part of the county when she took the census in 1920. When Wiley drove Old Brigham to Hawley on a courting venture, the ususally steady horse spooked and ran under the buggy, causing an ignominious first impression. When Glenn and Dalton transferred to Truby School for the upper grades, it was Brigham and the buggy that got them there. When it came time to break the land in the spring, Brigham pulled the plow.

Old Brigham had spirit about him—racing blood, some of them said. Tony, a half collie, was frustrated time and again when he chased along and could not stay up with Brigham. Mart was fond of training Old Brigham, putting him through paces that showed off his flair and alertness, but this made the horse harder to handle too. Once when Sula was sent leading Brigham to water, he went into his dance, causing her to throw down the reins and come under the fence despite all of Mart's exhortations for her to hold on.

When it occurred to him that Brigham would have to be traded soon or not at all, Mart announced his intention to sell the old animal. So strong was the family sentiment against this idea that even Mart had to back down this once. No sir, they told him, he's been too good a horse—Let's let him die right here where he's lived all these years. A few days before Old Brigham died, Glenn saw all of the horses together, racing across the field at a full gallop, Brigham out ahead of the rest.

It would hardly have been a farm at all without a few miscellaneous cats and dogs. They came and went over the years, only a few staying around long enough to become part of the family for any great length of time. One that did, though, was ol'Bounce, a playmate to several of the younger boys.

One of the finest dogs ever to run on the home place came under circumstances that were not strictly above board. His acquisition began with the illness of one of the children. When Dr. Stephens heard the symptoms described over the phone, he pretty well knew what was wrong and asked Mart to come over to the house and pick up some medicine. Mart took John and the auto and drove over to Dr. Stephens' house. While Mart was inside to get the medicine and visit with the doctor, John sat out in the car admiring Dr. Stephens' two fine young bulldogs. One of the pups was of a friendly disposition, yapping around outside the car door and playing as John waved his hand down and around alongside the window. Finally John opened the door and the dog jumped in and scrambled into the back seat, sat facing the windshield and ready to go. When Mart returned with the medicine, he drove on home as usual. Months later, when the dog had grown up, Dr. Stephens had occasion to make a house call at the Caffey place, and as he came in the front gate the bulldog all but ate him up.

Since just about everything had to be done by hand, there was never any shortage of work on the home place. Still, the biggest part of the work came in the growing season, when the young cotton plants had to be nurtured through to maturity and then picked and hauled to the gin. The task was a monumental one, and it didn't always proceed smoothly. There were various kinds of natural disasters that might interfere, like hail storms and droughts, or too much water at the wrong time. Misfortune was not uncommon. One spring the *Western Enterprise* reported the bad luck of one of the neighbors over near Pleasant Hill: "Gray Elliott had the misfortune of losing the best horse he had when his team ran away with his planter and one of them got his neck broken." If a crop could make it through the summer and fall to a good harvest, a farmer had much to be grateful for. To make a crop took both hard work and luck, and one without the other was not enough.

Once the land had been broken and planted, the real work could begin. As the cotton plants came out of the ground and began to leaf out and grow, weeds and Johnson grass grew up with them. In the days of the home place, there were no crop dusters or herbicides for getting rid of the weeds chemically. Some of the weeds could be taken out by running a cultivator over the rows—an implement with blades that swept the spaces between rows. But, then, as now, the only sure way of getting weeds out was to chop them out with a hoe. This chore was handled by Mart's children, each one hoeing his way along the rows for days at a time.

This was dull and tedious work, especially in the hot summer days. It was natural, then, that the boys should occasionally fall into some diversion when Mart was back at the house or off in town for the day. Wiley would pull one of the knotty green bolls and chunk it at Rudolph or John, or vice versa, and before you knew it bolls were flying across the rows in a furious volley, the boys ducking to the flimsy shelter of the cotton plants before standing to let fly a new barrage. If Mart came up and discovered the boys horsing around the green bolls wasted along the ground, there was trouble that began right there and ended behind the barn. Otherwise, the fight eventually played itself out and the work went on until quitting time.

When the open bolls were fluffy and ripe, all hands were in the field to pick them. Myra stayed at the house to cook and care for the babies, but anyone else who could drag a cotton sack was expected to be among the rows, stooped over, hands flying and the white bolls piling up in the big canvas bag behind. Young children helped, grown sons and daughters home for whatever reason helped.

One of the seasonal rituals of the home place was the morning when the picking was begun. On that morning

Myra stitched the cotton sacks, fashioning them from broad swaths of ducking material. She stitched the sacks one at a time on an old treadle Singer, tailoring each one to the size of the child awaiting its completion. Why the chore was invariably left to the last minute is not entirely clear. The sacks could have been made well ahead of time, all finished and ready for the time when they would be needed, but Myra always had other things to do. She stayed busy the year round with her other chores, until at last came the time when the sacks could be put off no longer. While she worked over the machine, the children stood by, each one waiting his turn. When a sack was finished Myra cast it aside to a waiting hand, and the child ran off to the field to begin the work.

Of the whole family, Mart and Bonnie came to be known as the best pickers. When Mart's cotton was out of the field, the family would sometimes hire out to pick for John Rice. Mart and Bonnie would each have four hundred pounds picked by four o'clock and go home while the others stayed until dark to pick as much or less.

*　　*　　*

There was not much privacy in a household that, over the years, included six boys and four girls, not counting Preston. It was a small and noisy house that held them all, and it was hard to have any of one's own business that did not end up being everybody else's. Whenever one of the boys said or did some fool thing, it was repeated over and over until everybody knew about it. Mischievous pranks could hardly be kept secret for long, and even courtship experiences were closely observed and soon were generally known among family members.

One idle afternoon Wiley and Rudolph lolled on the bedstead in the back room discussing some of the finer points concerning the subject of women, a matter of increasing curiosity and interest to them both. They shared their own recent adventures and jointly critiqued the girls

65

they knew of in the area, those of an interesting age. Eventually every aspect had been thrashed out and, with the topic exhausted, the two brothers moved on to some other subject.

From beneath the bed where they sprawled came a muffled clatter. The bedstead shuddered and a smaller boy scrooched his way out from underneath. Boyd scrambled to his feet, began to knock the dust off his clothes, and announced to his older brothers, "If that's all you're gonna say about women, I'll get out."

There wasn't much pampering done around the home place. With so many children underfoot and so much work to be done by hand each day, Myra hadn't the time to give patronizing attention to minor or imagined illnesses, and Mart had no patience with slackers. The children grew up to rely on themselves, to put bumps and sniffles aside and get on with work and play. One evening while Rudolph was out on one of the horses, it suddenly went skitterish and threw him. He hit hard on the ground and rolled around with an awful pain in his leg. Rudolph could hardly walk, the leg hurt so, and when the pain persisted severe and real, Mart took him to see the doctor. The neighborhood physician at this time was a man of average intelligence, just barely a doctor. He looked Rudolph over and felt around on the leg, and finally announced his prescription: "Go home and rub some sand on it," he said. "It'll be all right in a few days." Rudolph did as he was told. Many years later the leg gave way on a street in Denver. Rudolph's doctor had the leg X-rayed, and when the pictures came back, he was surprised by what he saw. "Did you ever break this leg before?" he asked. The bone, he explained, appeared to have been broken and never set to heal properly.

Meals were generally plentiful around the home place. Most foods were grown and prepared right at home. Myra's gardening and canning assured a steady supply of vegetables the year round. By dozens, the sealed Mason jars were stored in the dark underground cellar that also

66

provided shelter when storms threatened. Myra baked almost every day—biscuits, cornbread, loaves of light bread. For meat there was beef or pork, or Myra might kill a couple of young chickens and cut them up and fry them in the skillet. Not so plentiful were store bought goods. Canned tomatoes were a particular treat that came along only on special occasions. In general, Mart's family was hospitable and generous, but if neighbors happened to call just when the tomatoes were about to be served, the open cans were hidden behind the door until the visit was over and the company had gone.

From one end to the other, Mart and Myra's family spanned twenty-two years, from Olga, the oldest, to Glenn, the youngest. For the few years that all of the children were at home, mealtimes caused the dining room to bulge with so many crowded around the table, and a boy had to develop a good boarding house reach if he were to have anything to eat. Even so, there were times when the younger boys might have wished for a little higher place in the order of things. On Sundays Mart would sometimes invite another family home for dinner after preaching at the schoolhouse. When this happened, people had to be fed in as many as three sittings. The men and women and older children were fed first, then the younger children. Fried chicken was the standard fare for these gatherings, and by the time the third tableful sat down, the kids were lucky to have backs and wings and necks left to eat.

During the main years when all of the kids were around, space at the dinner table was at a premium. Mart's chair was at the head end. On one side Myra shared a corner of her chair with the littlest boy, Glenn, and other chairs were occupied by the older children. The middle children sat scrooched together on a bench along the other side. Boyd sat at the foot of the table on a homemade stool hammered together from scrap two by fours. Left without a place to sit at all was Dalton, who ate his meals standing up at the end of the table beside Boyd. No one was happier than Dalton when Bonnie married and moved out of the house, because he took her place and finally had a seat at the table.

As much food as a farm wife might put on the table, it was not easy to keep up with the appetites of cotton pickers and hog dressers and wood haulers. When neighbor children stayed for supper, the task could be almost hopeless. One evening some of the Caffey boys were invited to eat supper with the Rices, and despite the overload on Mrs. Rice's kitchen, John Rice was ever the gracious host. With every bowl scraped clean and not a scrap of food anywhere on the table, he leaned back in his chair at the end of the table and said in his casual, good natured way, "You boys make out your meal."

For most of the year, church meetings were plain and small, held at the schoolhouse. The Elliott community people didn't worry too much about denominations, all except for the Church of Christ people and some of the Baptists who didn't want to mix. The rest of the people went to church at the schoolhouse, sang hymns and listened to preaching if a preacher could be persuaded to come out from town or from one of the nearby country churches. Then in the early twenties, the Baptists built Unity Grove Church, just west of the schoolhouse. The church served fifteen years before finally folding for want of people.

The more ardent worshippers in south Jones County went to the Holiness tabernacle on the banks of the Clear Fork, near Phone Crossing. Here a broad tabernacle building had been erected—wide, but not so high, with a gently arched roof and solid walls along the sides. Here worship was not a spectator sport, but a spontaneous convulsion of prayer and praise. The worshippers vented their praises and their repentence as they were moved. On a mourners bench, the unwashed sinners pounded and wailed until all had been confessed and the cleansing power had been felt. There was plenty of demonstrative praise and shouting, especially when a new convert was led by the spirit to come down front.

The Pentecostals weren't the only ones who believed in a real God who was part of the day to day life in Jones County. The less vocal worshippers also had their occasional revivals and brush arbor meetings. Once a year, Preacher Copeland came into the Elliott community and evangelized for a solid week beneath a brush arbor built of heavy posts and thatched with branches. The meeting, held in late summer, brought a time of new spiritual intensity and left the country people with preachings they could ruminate on for weeks to come.

One summer Mart and Myra took the kids and drove over to Truby, to a revival at the Methodist Church. The country was in the grip of a terrible drought, and all of the farmers faced ruin and hoped for some kind of relief. In the course of the evening, the evangelist went to his knees and prayed for the rain that was needed. As the service broke up and people headed for home, thunderclaps burst in the night and the heavens broke loose. As Wiley told it, water poured from the skies and before Mart's family could get home, water was running up to the wagon bed. This story often provoked a certain amount of disbelief, but Wiley stood by it as long as he lived.

Some of the rural churches held singing schools and singing conventions at intervals throughout the year. These were times that brought country people together from all over the county, and they were times that Mart and his brothers looked forward to. A full fledged singing school lasted seven days and was led by a visiting teacher. For several years running, R.H. Cornelius came into the country in early April to lead the singing school at Stith, in the far southwest corner of Jones County. Cornelius taught music at the seminary in Fort Worth and edited the Cornelius gospel song books. He was widely revered among country singers all across Texas. When he came into Jones County, the little churches filled up with singers and with sound. Fletcher Caffey took a special pride in showing off his fine voice at these affairs, and he liked to be at his best. When he came up front to lead "I Know I'm Going

There," it was as beautiful a sound as came from any of the singers, R.H. Cornelius included.

For most of the year, life around the home place went on as usual. Work and schooldays and country pleasures occupied the Caffey boys for weeks at a time. The life was far from dull, what with so many brothers and sisters and neighbors around and so many amusements at hand. But once in a long while the children got a glimpse of the larger world when Mart took them to one of the bigger towns—to Abilene or perhaps even Fort Worth.

Once a year the circus came to Abilene, and if Mart could be coaxed, the whole family took two days away from the farm work and went to see it. In the early days, this was a long haul, made in a wagon or surrey. The way to Abilene took six hours or more in the days before autos, so Mart and the boys would have to be in the pasture by starlight looking for the horses. By the time they were harnessed and hitched and underway, daylight was breaking over east. By early afternoon, Mart was urging the horses down Pine Street toward Sharp's Wagon Yard. There the wagon was parked alongside those of the other country people who had come to town for the day and the horses were led away to be fed and watered and stabled. The afternoon and evening were spent in shopping and eyeballing the lastest new developments around Abilene, and in enjoying the fun of elephants and clowns and lion tamers and trapeze shows. When the circus was over the family bedded down in the wagonyard. In the morning there was time to finish any shopping chores, and then the horses were headed back north toward the home place.

These trips provided good times and supplied the kids with wonders and stunts that they would recall for months. They also afforded brief exposure to the city life and raised the possibility of undiscovered worlds beyond the Jones County line.

6. Mart Caffey

Around Mart Caffey's farm there was hardly ever any doubt as to who was in charge. All through the main years of the home place, for as long as he lived, Mart made the rules and gave the orders. Mart bossed the kids through their days of farm work and laid down his commandments concerning right conduct around the house. When the sons and daughters remembered their childhood times in later years, they never spoke of things happening because "Mama and Papa talked it over," or because "We had a family meeting and decided." Rather it was usually because, "Papa, he always had the idea that . . ." Myra had her own favorite interests for the family and her ways of seeing many of them fulfilled, but Mart plainly ran the household pretty much the way he wanted. Once he had adopted his own particular set of facts and aims and principles, he held to them through the years and over the decades. When Mart stood fast for some principle of right or integrity, he did so with a rigid certainty that rendered all opposition futile. When he made a mistake in judgment, he did that too with the same righteous certainty. He was hardly ever vague or hesitant.

Mart had plenty of joviality about him; he had a big belly laugh that came easy and carried deep and resonant all through the house. He also had his pleasures—the tricks with Brigham, the singing conventions around Jones County, the sociable trading days in Anson. But where work was concerned, Mart would not be distracted. He knew his aims and committed his efforts accordingly, year upon year. Mart could forego the goodtiming and immediate pleasures for which some of the neighbors gave their time and money. Instead, Mart put his labors into his farm and family, and as the decades passed, he saw many of his aims substantially fulfilled. Mart worked hard and he worked his kids hard. He cut a bold figure through life, and the sons and daughters learned much from his example—ways to emulate and ways to steer clear of.

Mart was a stern disciplinarian, and the boys did not lightly cross his path. However, there were occasions when constant obedience got to be too much and the boys would have to pull some stunt—perhaps to show that they were live and separate individuals after all. There is no indication that Mart genuinely detested the occasional misbehavior; on the contrary, he seems to have enjoyed the spunk and liveliness that it demonstrated. All the same, he would not let these small acts of insubordination go unpunished. Mart knew how to make good use of a rope or leather strap. With a peach tree switch he could set you on fire. Cotton boll fights and schoolday picnics seem to have been responsible for a good many of the whippings. It can be said that the boys ordinarily did not get themselves whipped without at least having had some good fun to show for it.

One Saturday Menco Rice stayed over to spend the night in the back room with the Caffey boys. As the house settled for the night, Wiley, Rudolph, and Menco lay plotting a scheme for hightailing to Anson to see some western adventure at the silent picture show. When all was quiet through the house and Mart's snore signalled safety, they slipped out of the room and stole away into the pasture to gather in three horses. By starlight the boys bridled and saddled the stodgy old workhorses and lit out for town.

Far up into the night, the boys returned from their adventure. They unsaddled the horses and turned them out to pasture, crept into the house and took their usual places. When daylight broke and Mart went out to do the milking, he was not happy to find his horses flecked with lather and the bridles damp and sweaty. Back at the house, Mart went busting into the boys' room as he often did to get them up and going with the sun. Mart let out a big laugh. "Wiley and Rudolph, did you all have a good time last night? I'll see you right after breakfast." When the boys were through picking at their plates, they rose from the table and followed to the barn to pay for their night's folly at the action end of a hemp rope.

It is really hard to exaggerate the extent to which Mart's dominance was ingrained in his relationships with the kids. His word was law around the house, and this was a fundamental premise in all his dealings with the boys.

Sometime after the new house was built, there came a dreary night of low clouds, pitch dark, and drizzle. The countryside was saturated and murky streamlets ran in every row and ditch. It was a night for burrowing in under a pile of quilts and staying there. The family lay sleeping, the house quiet for the night. Sleeping in the back room were the three younger boys—Boyd, Dalton, and Glenn. Boyd, the oldest of the three, was now about fifteen years old. In the middle room were the girls—any who happened to be home. And in the front room was the big iron bedstead where Mart and Myra slept.

Along toward midnight an automobile shimmied up the road, its headlights finding a way in the night. The drizzle had let up by now, but the clay surface of the little country road was yet slippery and bar ditches ran muddy to either side of the narrow roadway. The vehicle crept past the house and made its way a little farther up the road to the east, then slid off into the ditch. Several tries at gunning the engine and spinning the wheels made it plain that the car was genuinely stuck. The neighbor woman driving stepped down into the muck and slogged back up the road to seek Mart Caffey's help.

"Mr. Caffey!" she called out from the road. It took several tries before anyone could be aroused. In time, Mart raised himself up in the bed and gave his attention to the distant voice outside his window.

"Mr. Caffey!" she shouted again, "do you have a dog?"

"No," he called back, "What do you want with a dog?"

73

As a matter of fact, the woman didn't want a dog at all, but only to know whether she might safely walk up into the yard. There was no dog on the place at this time, so she approached to tell Mart of her predicament and her need to be getting on home if he could lend a hand and haul her auto out of the ditch.

Mart was ready to oblige, as any good neighbor would have been, but he saw no need to rouse himself from the bed—not with three boys in the back room. He bellowed for Boyd. One of the boys woke and punched Boyd into consciousness, enough so that he could answer. Mart called out his instructions, telling Boyd to get out and bring up the team and go with the woman. This was no small request, given the kind of night it was and the fact that the horses might be clear in the back of the pasture, a half-mile or more away.

Boyd's head was full of sleep. He was awake only enough to hear the instructions and to know who they were coming from. He called back in reply, "Do you want me to put on my pants?"

With respect to the farm work, Mart went hard at it every day, and he expected the boys to stay up with him. To Mart, as to many of the neighbors, work was a virtue as well as a means to sustenance. It was, along with certain other qualities, the measure of a man. Mart disparaged laziness, spoke with disdain about neighbors and in-laws who seemed content just to get along from year to year doing as little as possible. Mart determined early that no child of his would grow up idle or lazy.

Mart's kids had work to do the year round. Usually they worked at home, but if things were caught up in Mart's field and some neighbor needed help, they were occasionally allowed to hire out at the going rate of fifty or seventy-five cents a day. They chopped weeds for Haskell Caffey, picked cotton for John Rice, sometimes helped kinfolks who needed help but couldn't afford to pay.

Some of the boys had their suspicions that Mart purposely connived to make extra work for them, just for the sake of seeing that they were kept busy. In cultivating the rows of cotton, Mart never tried to make an especially clean job of it, as Dalton felt he could have done. Instead, he left an unturned strip between each two rows, so that weeds were sure to grow up among the cotton plants causing untold days of labor for the boys.

There was generally a lull in the natural demands of the farm work between weed chopping time in midsummer and cotton picking time in the fall. Mart filled this time easily by having the boys cut and stack stovewood and do other odd jobs around the house and barn. He didn't believe in slack time.

During the school term, free hours were soon filled with chores of Mart's devising. Early and late there was milking to be done. Hogs had to be slopped and the cattle and mules and horses fed and tended. During two different winters, Mart hired Mexicans to grub out acres of new ground for cultivation. The hired men cut the downed trees into stovewood and stacked the wood in cords. To the younger boys Mart assigned the chore of hauling the wood in from the back eighty and stacking it near the house. This was to be done after school and on Saturdays.

Even on rainy days, Mart wanted to see people working. He could often think of legitimate tasks and set the kids to work on them. When no idea occurred to him right off or when the boys balked at some extreme measure, Mart fumed around the house pacing out his impatience and citing his own younger days when the work had gone on no matter what the weather. "In Mississippi," he liked to recall, "we'd be in the barn makin' shuck collars." Shuck collars were the homemade horse collars that the Mississippi hill farmers had fashioned for want of manufactured leather collars or the money to buy them. After a tubular structure had been stitched of canvas, it was stuffed with cornshucks. Then the two ends were stitched together. The result was a padded ring that went over the head of a horse or mule to cushion its shoulders against the drag of a plow or planter of wagon pulled behind. For as long as Mart's children could remember, he had always bought good manufactured collars in town. "What good would shuck collars do us here?" one of the boys would sometimes ask. There was no good answer to this, and Mart could only simmer down and bristle under the irritation of seeing the boys while away the day.

Thrift was an ever present element in Mart's character. Again, it was not just a matter of practicality, but one of virtue as well. In his earliest years, Mart made a habit of working and doing without and saving, of putting his efforts into long term gains and not spending them away on good times and frills. Mart could point to plenty of examples where waste and frivolity and reliance on credit had been ruinous, and he resolved never to fall victim. Mart's family would make their own or do without before they would live beyond their means. Mart was loath to go into debt for any reason, and he did so with great reluctance and discomfort, and only on rare occasions. The point was driven home to the children over and over again: "Don't buy anything until you've got the money to pay for it." This may not in fact have represented the ultimate wisdom in financial management, but it served Mart well enough. While his brothers went along about the same from year to year, Mart gradually accumulated a little more land and a few of the newest inventions and conveniences until, without owing anyone, he was clearly the most prosperous of the four. When hard times came with the "Twenty Break" and later with the Great Depression, neighbors all around lost their farms for having dallied around on mortgages for too many years while their money went into more appealing pleasures of the moment. But Mart was able to weather the times, his own land long since fully paid for.

There were some good years for the farming enterprise, but on the whole, Mart learned not to count on steadiness or prosperity from one year to the next. Cotton might bring a good price today, go begging at half the price in a few short months or years. Money didn't come easy and Mart didn't let go of it easy. He didn't give money to the kids at all, the single exception being Christmas. At Christmas each child received, along with an apple and an orange and nuts, a shiny dime, which always came accompanied by the admonition, "Don't spend it all in one place." Myra might occasionally give her children butter or eggs to sell for enough to see the picture show in Anson, and sometimes they could earn money working for a neighbor, but Mart didn't give them money.

Mart's practice of economy was greatly enhanced by his knack for trading, although he never used this talent to full advantage. Mart could always take livestock or equipment of some kind to town and come home with something better. It came natural to him. There were men who made trading a full time vocation, and Mart could have done this too, had he chosen to do so. Mart could have made a million dollars trading around over the country, but the prospect was not one that appealed to him. The family was Mart's first priority, and he would not tolerate the long spells away from home that the trading life required. Mart also felt that trading carried with it something of a stigma for shadiness and a real temptation toward crookedness. A good trade by its very nature meant coming out ahead. This often involved getting the better of a less wary or assertive man. It was too easy, Mart felt, to slide on into greed and deceitfulness, and this Mart would not have. "Avoid the very appearance of evil," he would tell the children, quoting a Bible verse that he had absorbed. So Mart kept his penchant for trading in the background, used it only in the course of buying and selling lots of cattle for the farm, bargaining for household items, getting work accomplished when money was short.

Mart always had ways of getting things done without putting out any money. In the early years he was usually looking to clear out a little more of the shinnery and put more land in cultivation. This was not something that had to be done right now, but a task that could wait until opportunity might knock. When a wandering Indian man

071720 Howard County Library
Big Spring, Texas

came up the road one day looking for work, Mart struck a bargain with him and set him to work grubbing out several acres in exchange for a heifer calf. When "T" Caffey needed firewood one winter, Mart happened to have a surplus from some recent clearing he had done on his land. Mart provided several loads of wood and took his payment in days of farm labor during the following season. When Mart's weeds were about to get out of hand, he called on "T" and had him bring some of his dozen children and chop the field clean. When Mart finally traded for a tractor up in the 1930s, he put up his old implements, along with an assortment of horses and mules. He bargained for a tractor and finally struck a deal, having put out only about a hundred dollars cash. Mart was a good trader.

Mart Caffey looked after his business about as well as any man in Jones County. He kept track of what he had and of what he had spent on particular crops or lots of livestock. Ever so often Mart would feed out a bunch of cattle on the pasture grass or field stalks. When they were ready for market Mart and his nephew Tom went around over the country buying up cattle until they had filled out a car load. Then the two men drove their herd to the railroad, loaded them onto a cattle car, and rode with them to Fort Worth and the Daggett-King Commission House. In a coat pocket Mart carried the black book in which each expense and each credit was recorded. When the cattle were weighed and sold, Mart knew right away what he had made on them.

Mart kept track of his trades, knew his obligations and his rights, knew what was his and what wasn't. When a neighbor dared to encroach by moving the boundary fence ten feet over onto his Truby land, Mart took exception. Armed with a shovel and his abstract to the property, Mart walked out the perimeter, noting landmarks that proved the validity of the old fenceline. Then he sought out his neighbor and stated his business: "I want this fence put back where it belongs right now. I'm not goin' to have you fightin' with my wife and kids about this after I'm dead."

Within a few days the fence was back in its old place.

Singing was one of Mart's great pleasures. He grew up singing back in Mississippi, where there was always plenty of lusty singing in the little country churches. To the hill people, singing was not to be taken for granted, but learned, cultivated, and enjoyed for long hours at a time. In singing schools of several days duration, people were taught to count rhythm and to read shape notes. All day singing conventions brought country people from far and wide for a succession of rousers and "specials"—quartets, duets, and the like. When the southern people moved westward, all of this came with them, so that the same kinds of events now took place in Jones County, usually with Mart and one or more of his brothers in attendance. For a time, Mart and Fletcher and Olga and Bonnie made a quartet, practiced and offered special numbers at some of the singing days.

Mart sang tenor, and as with everything else, he did it his own way. He never quite mastered the skill of finding the right notes and words all at the same time when reading over the tops of his spectacles to follow the tenor line on an unfamiliar piece of music. His rendition, then, came out as a strong if somewhat stumbling mix of words and syllables. Peering at the book over the wire rims, Mart would lift his voice over the notes: "Dr-tm-be-fa-sol-fa-doo, Jesus-upta-fa-sa-say, Lead-me-su-sa-me-fa-sol-d the blessed way . . ."

Once Mart had begun to get ahead in Jones County, one of his first acquisitions for the household was an upright piano. Mart left with some of the boys early one morning and drove to Abilene, taking along an old wagon and a team of horses that had outlived their best working years on the farm. Mart did his bargaining and finally traded even—the wagon and team for the piano. By nightfall he was home with the big upright. It stood in the front room of the old house, and then of the new house, the center of many good singing times. The piano stayed on the home place for over forty years, burned up with the house in the years after Myra had left the farm for good.

"I just like music," Mart used to say, "I don't care if it's not anything but somebody pickin' on a splinter." This would seem to be a pretty all encompassing endorsement, and in general, it was true. There were, however, certain exceptions. Mart was convinced that anyone who played the guitar could come to no good. He could point to particular kinfolks whose kids had taken up the guitar and thereafter never worked another day. It seemed to Mart that these people just naturally fell to lolling around and plunking and strumming, having lost all ambition and all discipline for work. The pursuit of stringed instruments was, therefore, discouraged.

The religion-centered upbringing that John and Nancy Caffey provided back in Mississippi rubbed off on all of their four sons, deeply ingrained throughout their lives. Mart was a church going man and, like his brothers, he knew so many scriptures so well that they were bound to surface whenever they seemed to explain particular events of daily life. Too, Mart carried dozens of the old hymns in his head, sang them not only at brush arbor meetings and singing conventions, but at his work around the farm as well. One of the regular sounds of the home place was the familiar tenor voice carried from off in the distance, singing the strains of some old favorite: "I want to be a worker for the Lord, I want to trust and speak his holy word. I will work, I will pray, I will labor every day, in the vineyard of the Lord."

Photographs

A Jones County Album

John T. Caffey, farmer and circuit preacher; Prentiss County, Mississippi. About 1890. From a tintype.

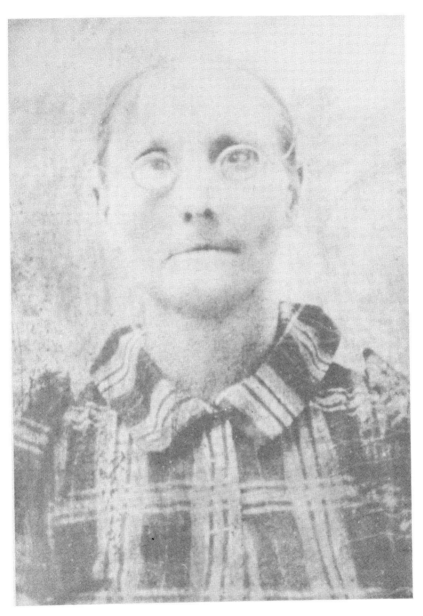

Nancy Thomas Caffey, wife of John T. Caffey. Tintype.

Shady Grove Methodist Church; Prentiss County, Mississippi.

Farm cabin of John T. Caffey.

Cabin in the Shady Grove community; Prentiss County, where Myra Lollar grew up. Boyd is the man in the picture, taken on the 1925 summer trip.

Uncle Edgar's big family. Three girls are missing, not yet born. Picture made about 1895.

Mart and Myra, Viola, Bonnie, Olga, John. About 1897.

Uncle Oscar and Aunt Dealie, Lila and Lillian.

Uncle Fletcher and Aunt Mary.

Church meeting at Elliott Schoolhouse, about 1912. Mart is in the center of the picture. Myra and Dalton are the mother and child. Note the long, light colored "Sacred Harp" song books. The two men peeking around the corner of the building on the right were left out of the picture because they had been drinking.

Elliott school, about 1912. Sixth and seventh from left on the front row are Wiley and Rudolph Caffey. Fifth from left on the second row is John. Second from left, third row, Viola. Third from right, top row, Sula. The teacher is Mr. Spillman.

Myra and Glenn. About 1915.

Viola, Alma Bronson, and Bonnie at Stamford College, about 1915.

Viola.

Mart and Myra, about 1916, in front of the old house.

Boyd, about 1915. The mail order soldier suit was too small. Boyd put it on only long enough to make the picture, then it was packed up and sent back to Sears Roebuck.

Dalton on the front steps, about 1916. He had been slapped away from the dinner table.

Glenn, about 1916.

Olga, Viola, Sula, Bonnie.

Glenn and Bounce, about 1918.

Bonnie took nurses' training at the Alexander Sanitarium in Abilene.

Bonnie and John, about 1916.

Bonnie, about 1918, taking the train back to Missouri after a visit home. This was the last that the family saw Bonnie.

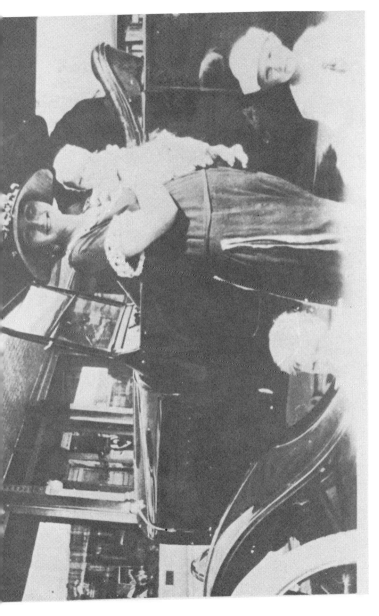

Sula and three of her children. About 1918.

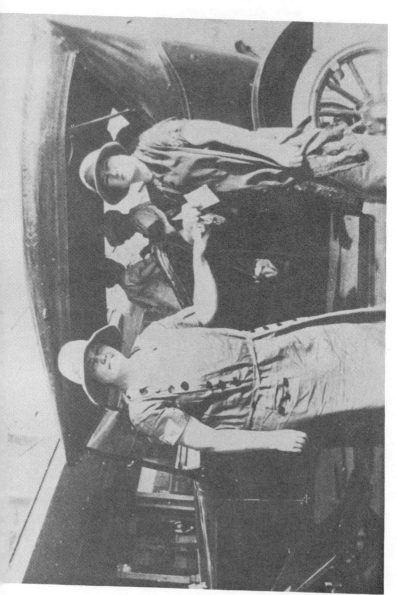

Olga and Viola.

Viola and the old house.

Mart and Mr. Lindsey, Mart's old house.

Myra, Mart, Viola, Dalton. About 1923.

The new house, about 1924. Note stairwell to the cellar at left and outhouse behind the cellar.

Uncle Oscar, Aunt Dealie, Aunt Mary, Uncle Fletcher, about 1936.

Mart and Myra, about 1940.

Rudolph on stage in New York, about 1940.

Wiley, Mart, Viola's daughter Sue, about 1940.

Myra, about 1954.

7. Shenanigans

Someone who knew boys once had this to say about their value in accomplishing work: "If you've got one boy, you've got one boy. If you've got two boys, you've got half a boy. And if you've got three boys, you don't have any boys at all." Whenever Mart was around to supervise the farm work, he could generally keep his boys working pretty steady. Nonetheless, he would have understood the remark and its comment on the chemistry of boys together. Mart hardly ever had fewer than three boys on the home place, and together they could stir up some outlandish capers. Occasional cotton boll fights were to be expected, as were skirmishes with neighbor boys and days of playing hookey from school. Other stunts were of a more novel sort.

When the picture show came to Anson, a whole new interest was born for the farm boys. Come Saturday night there was hardly a more appealing place to be than sitting in the darkened movie house in Anson, eyes glued to the screen while jerky flashes of light reflected outward into the seats and Tom Mix rode hard across the screen to capture a bandit or rescue some fair miss. Along with the feature there was usually a serial—"The Perils of Pauline" or some similar epic. These were of the kind in which a week's episode would inevitably end with the stage coach teetering on a cliff or a thundering band of Indians descending on the hero and a few frightened settlers. When the heart pounding action suddenly turned to a blank screen and "Come Back Next Week for the Next Exciting Episode," the protagonist was always on the brink of disaster.

If Mart was willing, the Caffey boys could gather up a

bunch of eggs to sell in town for the ten cent admission and a bag of popcorn, and off they would go. This was not an every week privilege, however, so the boys were often left disappointed and burdened with an unbearable curiosity about the fate of the hero in the latest serial. By hook or crook, they found ways of staying up with the most recent perils and heroics.

One of the advantages of the divided house was that the kids could get away with a little more carrying on than if their noise were closer to their parents' room. As it was, they could pull off night adventures without so much danger of being detected at all, unless someone told. When the boys needed to know what was happening at the picture show, they would wait until the house was quiet, Mart and Myra sleeping up front in the main part of the house. Then Wiley was sent riding into Anson on old Flag. By bedtime a bucket of eggs would have been gathered and secreted away in some safe place—a dozen for the movie admission and one or two extras in case one was broken along the way. Wiley would saddle old Flag and ride off to town to see the show, filing away every important detail for retelling. When he came in home around midnight or one o'clock, the rest of the kids shook off their sleep and came awake, ready to hear what had happened this week. They got down in the floor and gathered around while Wiley recounted each bit of action.

They say that no worthwhile task is easy. There are some other challenges that are not so easy either, but that also are not particularly worthwhile. Some feats just have to be attempted for sport or in order to show someone else that it can be done. Like all good boys, Mart's sons had to try some of these. Why else would Wiley have taken off down the road in Fess Neal's car when he had seen few cars before and didn't know the first thing about driving one? Why else would a boy brave Bob White's dog to make off with a watermelon under each arm when plenty were available at home?

Along with their other sports, the Caffey boys liked to

try their hands at riding the unbroken calves that came on the place. Once Mart had a bull calf that none of the boys could ride. With all the chores done and an idle hour to spend before suppertime, the boys were down in the lot giving it their durndest again. Wiley tried to ride and couldn't stay on. Rudolph got on and was promptly pitched into the fence. Menco Rice didn't want to go near the animal. Finally John said, "Tie my feet under him." The others took a piece of rope and bound John's feet together underneath the calf's belly, so that his legs were fastened around the calf. The younger boys finished tying and stepped back and away they went. The calf bolted and John snapped backward, then pitched forward to catch up with the momentum of the mad calf. The calf ran panic stricken around the lot, then headed straight for a feed trough that sat a few feet off the ground on posts. The calf darted under and John slammed head-on into the trough, ended up in a flailing heap of arms and legs with the bawling calf.

Once in a while two of the boys would tangle in a brief but earnest scuffle. One day Wiley and Rudolph were at it out east of the house, tumbling this way and that in a shallow draw that ran down through the field. Whenever Rudolph engaged in these tussles, he was apt to put up a good fight until, all at once, he had had enough. When Rudolph was ready to quit, he would slack off and roll out of the clinch, come up weary and exclaim his fatigue: "Oh, Lawdy mercy me." This time Wiley laid the younger boy to the ground with a bone jarring blow that settled the struggle, but good. "Oh, Lawdy mercy me, boys," Rudolph wailed, "you've busted my kidneys loose from my back."

Wiley was a sleepwalker. When he sat up in bed and then stood to walk out the door, there was no telling where he was apt to end up. He slept in his shirttail, as all of the boys did. When they went to bed, the boys just pulled off their overalls and lay down to sleep in their shirts and shorts.

One evening Wiley had one of his spells and rose from the bed to walk out into the yard. He wandered out the gate and walked east along the road toward Elliott Schoolhouse. As it happened, a revival service was underway at the school on this particular evening, and a good many of the neighbors were gathered there. Wiley continued up the road and was almost to the schoolhouse when the preacher came to the fever pitch of his sermon and began to shout. As Wiley came awake the meeting ended and the crowd began to break up, neighbor folks heading for their buggies to start home. With neighbors pulling out onto the road, Wiley discovered his fix—out in the open in his shirt and undershorts. Wiley scrambled over the barbed wire fence and took to the open country of his father's field. He made his way home along the crop rows under cover of darkness and safely out away from the road.

In summer the boys often bedded down on the screened in porch that ran along the back of the house. Summer nights were warm enough as it was, and inside the house they could be miserable. Rather than lay sweating in the room, the boys would take and toss their mattresses flat on the porch deck where gentle breezes came across from the north.

Up in the night one summer, Mart lay drowsy and chanced to hear a big, wet "kerplunk," deep and heavy, as from the depths of the cistern. To be on the safe side, Mart crawled from the bed and walked to the back door, opened it and counted the kids asleep on the breezeway. One was missing, and it was Wiley. Mart woke the household and set it in a dither. "Wiley fell in the cistern," he hollered, heading straightway for the side of the house.

Mart climbed over into the cistern well and took hold of the rope, lowered himself into the pitch dark shaft. When Mart reached bottom and dangled in the water, he found only the family cat paddling around, its hair all slick and matted. Mart toted it along and made his way back up

119

to the surface, climbed out onto the ground. Out behind the house was Wiley, oblivious to the hubbub, walking around the yard in his sleep.

Sometimes neighbor families fell victim to stunts perpetrated by the Caffey boys. Sometimes the neighbors knew who had done the deed, and sometimes they didn't.

One cold winter when the woodpile ran low, Mart took a notion to build it back up *right now*. On a Saturday afternoon he sent Boyd and one of the other boys to take the wagon down to the deep shinnery place near Uncle Fletcher's farm. The boys were not keen for the chore but, the order having been issued, they hitched up the team and drove off down the road toward the shinnery place.

The brothers could not get down to work. They were drawn to other curiosities, lulled into idle games. They frittered the afternoon away until, at once, they were aware of the sun drawn low on the horizon and the wagon yet rattling empty. With the realization upon them, the boys called upon all of their inventiveness, for they did not dare to drive in home without the wood. It was at this moment that they thought of their neighbor, Bob Carter, and of his penchant for staying well ahead of his chores. They set the team east and rumbled along the lane, pulled up before the Carter place. Before them was the woodpile, big as a house and not a soul around. The boys pulled alongside and piled the wagon high, rolled away east and finally drove in home with the big load that would last all winter.

John was something of a prankster. He enjoyed a good laugh, enjoyed poking at people's foibles and obstrenities. He was amused by the proud and silly way in which the Halls—Henry and Willie—regarded their hunting hounds.

Henry and Willie Hall lived on the same piece of property, Henry up away from the river a half mile and Willie down nearer the banks in a house his father had helped him build when Willie married. The father and son continued to work side by side and to enjoy sporting times together.

One morning John picked up the phone and rang Willie Hall's number. When Willie answered, John put on his best imitation of Henry's tinny, high pitched voice: "Willie—Willie, this is Papa. Willie, Old Bessie is mighty sick this morning, she's mighty sick. I think you'd better come up here." Willie was all concerned and alarmed. He took the bait and responded ever so gullibly as John went on playing the part of Henry Hall. As the conversation went on, Henry Hall chanced to pick up the phone to call Willie and, the party line being an open affair, he dropped right in on the dialogue between John and Willie. Henry didn't know who the perpetrator was, but he did recognize the mocking rendition of his own voice and he soon got the drift of the conversation. Red-faced mad, he broke in to give the caller a piece of his mind. "You couldn't have been born," he barked into the phone, "you must have been hatched out of a stump."

Parties were held occasionally at farmhouses around the Elliott community. These gatherings were primarily for the benefit of the older boys and girls who were coming into the age of mutual attraction and interest. The young people played various games, many of them designed to facilitate pairing and hand-holding. Sometimes the boys and girls played "Snap," a game in which the players sat in a circle while one of the girls walked around the outside to choose the boy of her fancy. When the girl snapped her fingers over the boy's head, he was to give chase around the circle. The girl would run, feigning an attempt to escape, slowing down a little if necessary to make certain of the boy catching her. Then the couple went outside to hold hands and enjoy a moment to themselves.

When Rudolph finished all the schooling available at Elliott and Pleasant Hill, he made plans for going off to attend Simmons Academy in Abilene, as Wiley had done before him. When the time drew near, neighbor kids were invited to a party at the home place for a time of fun and good wishes. The year would have been about 1920. Myra had bought Rudolph a new suit in Anson, and he wore it proudly on the evening of the party.

As the party went along, the younger brothers hung around close enough to watch and snicker. Out east of the house, just out of the way, were Dalton and Boyd and two of the neighbor boys, Bryant Myers and Roy Shirley. The younger boys were old enough to understand the object of "Snap" and of their brothers' early efforts at courting, but young enough at the same time to regard them with irreverence and teasing. Because Rudolph was so obviously and outwardly peeved at their devilment, the young boys especially liked to make him aware of their presence whenever he stepped out onto the porch with a girl. They deviled him persistently through the evening, and finally Rudolph's patience gave way. Rudolph bolted from the porch and charged the hecklers, coming on a tear to put an end to the harassment. Only one thing stopped Rudolph from giving his younger brothers a well deserved beating. What Rudolph had forgotten was the barbed wire fence that stood between him and the boys. He hit it full tilt, tumbled sky wester'n crooked, hit the ground in a heap with the new suit torn to pieces.

Mart had a few rules around the house. One of these was that all alcoholic drinks were strictly forbidden, the single exception being the bottle that he kept on hand for the occasional social visits of certain neighbor friends. Whenever a good friend came to the house and Mart was inclined to offer him a snort, the two men would go off out of the way—the bottle was never opened in the house or around the children.

One evening when Glenn was a boy of about ten years old, the family sat down to supper and found that the jar of preserves then on the table had about been scraped clean. Glenn, being the youngest and therefore subject to the most menial errands, was sent to the cellar to fetch a new jar. Glenn went outside to the cellar, laid back the heavy door, and descended the steps to the dark shelves of canned goods. Glenn peered over the various cans of fruits and vegetables and came face to face with the bottle of whiskey. Glenn had never tasted whiskey, so he uncorked the bottle, laid his head back, and took a good, long pull on the bottle. The taste of the hard liquor took Glenn by surprise, kicked him silly as it went down. It was hot and rough. Glenn recovered his senses, put the bottle back on the shelf and took the jar of preserves for which he had been sent.

When Glenn took his place at the supper table, he was loose and giddy. The next morning Myra went to the cellar and moved the bottle to a new keeping place.

1920 was the year of the government's ten year census and one of the years of the national experiment known as Prohibition. When the Census Bureau started up its machinery to count the people in Jones County, Viola gained temporary employment as a census enumerator. By horse and buggy, she drove all over south Jones County, stopping at houses along the country lanes to fill in the long census blanks and ask questions of the farm people. All day long Viola made her way among the backroads. At day's end, she could usually be invited to spend the night at some farm where she was given supper and a bed. This was the way of it among the country people in the days before motels and autos.

When the job was finished and Viola was back home to stay, she recounted her experiences and told of the people she had met in her travels. Viola told of one evening when she was taken in by a nice family and treated particularly well. She didn't know the people well, but the man's name was Boyd. One thing that puzzled Viola, though, was the noise she had heard in the night. For a long spell she had heard people out back moving things around. When Mart heard the tale, he came alive. "Why, didn't you know who that was? That's ol' Slicker Boyd—he's a bootlegger."

*   *   *

Mart's family didn't by any means have a monopoly on shenanigans. All of the Mississippi brothers had grown up to have fun about them, and it had its way of coming out.

For the most part, Fletcher Caffey stayed to himself and left other people in peace. Fletcher had a good bit of wit about him, but he wouldn't ordinarily use it against another man unless provoked.

Fletcher sometimes made trips to Abilene during his early years in Jones County. Whenever he made the long drive by wagon and team, the natural first stop was Sharp's Wagon Yard, where all of the country men stopped to leave their animals. Sharp's Wagon Yard became the natural place for congregating and for sharing news and gossip and long, windy tales, and a group of farm men could usually be found doing just that.

One of the regulars around the wagon yard was a man who seemed to have no other real occupation. He hung around day in and day out, listening in on most of the bull sessions and bumming chewing tobacco off the other men. He never seemed to have his own tobacco.

One morning as Fletcher walked across the mud-chewed yard, he happened upon a weatherbeaten plug of tobacco, still in its faded wrapper, long since trampled into the lot. Fletcher reached down for the plug and filed it away in a coat pocket. Later in the day, the freeloader sidled up to him and made his pitch: "Fletcher, let me have a chaw of your tobacco." Fletcher reached in the pocket and pulled out the plug, yanked off a generous hunk and gave it to the man. The fellow stuck the wad in his jaw and walked away, his mouth filling up with a foul taste. After a few minutes he got rid of the tobacco and told the other railbirds, "That Fletcher Caffey—he chews the *meanest* tobacco."

Oscar and Dealie came from Mississippi in 1902 with four girls and an older boy. Two more girls were born in Texas. They were a freewheeling bunch.

Oscar himself was good humored and jolly—not at all a worrier. He could take life as it came, enjoy the good times and let the rest of it go. He liked being around people and stirring up laughs, and he did so easily and naturally. Oscar farmed at Truby and later at the Union community, but he always had enterprises going on the side. He grew watermelons and sold them at Merkel, kept old "First Monday" horses and took them to trading days in Anson. The first Monday of each month was the day the country men came to town bringing along goods and livestock with which to bargain for other goods. First Monday horses were ones that had seen better days, and their main value was that they gave Oscar a reason to be in Anson to share in the drinking and sociability of the trading times.

Oscar never made or lost much on first Mondays, but he had good times and came to know a great many people in Jones County. One election year Oscar took a notion to run for the office of County Commissioner. While the neighbors found Oscar affable enough, they apparently didn't judge him the one best suited to stewardship of their public business. He lost badly. In one voting precinct Oscar got no votes at all and earned the nickname, "Goose Egg Caffey."

Dealie was plainspoken and sometimes a little bit ornery. She came by these traits honestly, her own father having been a rough talker all his life. When Dealie's mother died back in Mississippi, her father and brother came to Texas to live with Oscar and Dealie.

Old man Jones didn't change his way of talking for anybody, so the little girls around Oscar's house grew up learning expressions that other small girls didn't learn. One morning Mart and John drove over to Oscar's place on some small errand. As they turned up the lane toward the house, Florence came running to meet the buggy. Mart reined the horses to a stop and Florence raced up aglow and panting to blurt out, "Uncle Mart, Uncle Mart—we got a new baby and her name is Lillian." Mart made over the news appropriately and continued up the lane with Florence running alongside. Myrtle saw the buggy and raced from the porch. She came running out of breath and full of news: "Uncle Mart—we got a new baby and her name is Lillian." At this Florence was acutely peeved. She spun on her sister and made a defiant face toward the younger girl: "Eye God," she scowled, "I done told 'im."

Oscar's girls were used to saying whatever they pleased. Oscar pretty well let them alone, gave them little to fear. One afternoon during maize cutting season a dark cloud blew in from the north and one of the girls came in to tell Florence her father's instructions: "Papa says for you to take the wagon and bring that feed out of the field." Florence didn't appreciate the message and stated her mind: "Papa ain't too purty to haul that feed himself."

The kids could get away with just about anything. John, the only boy, was one of the area rowdies, good at starting a ruckus and getting out of the way, leaving the finishing of it to someone else. One morning John was horsing around in the house, climbing and crawling among the rafters. When Dealie walked into the room John dropped out of the alcove and jumped down on her shoulders. When she went to get mad, he begged off as usual: "Oh Mama, I just wanted to love you."

Aunt Dealie had a great fear of dark clouds. When a cloud blew up in the north sky she wasted no time in gathering up the kids and herding them all into the cellar. Her brother, Bill Jones, was not so eager to go. He was fascinated by the boiling clouds, preferred to lay out on the grassy knoll near the house and watch the storm roll in. "Well all right then," Dealie would tell him, "you just lay out there and get blown away." He didn't though, he lived to die a natural death. Dealie did too, at the age of ninety-four.

8. Accumulatin'

For quite a few years Mart stayed on the leading edge of progress in Jones County. Mart was always careful with his money, though not in a miserly way. Rather than spend it away on extravagances or good times, he wanted to put in into more lasting pleasures. Once established on the home place, Mart continued to make regular improvements and acquisitions, gradually improving his situation and increasing his worth over the years. Mart was generally among the first to have each new convenience that made its way from the industrial northeast to the byways of the shinnerylands. He never amassed any sort of empire or fortune, nor did he have any inclination to do so. But Mart and Myra saw that their children were provided for as well as any in the Elliott community and gave them an upbringing that pointed them toward the future even as it was steeped in ways of the past.

In the early years, two pieces of land were added to the quarter section that Mart and Myra had on the home place. Depending on which family members were around for a given season, the tracts could be farmed by family or rented to sharecroppers.

In the summer of 1907, Uncle Edgar bought a hundred acre parcel from Mr. Rowell—a sandy land farm a mile north of Truby on the road toward Anson. This was one of the few times in his life that Edgar had ever taken a notion to own land. By December he had thought better of the commitment, and he sold the land to Mart for cash. Thereafter the place provided a grubstake for various sons and daughters who were grown and ready to farm.

In the last years of their lives, Myra's parents left the country around the home place and moved to a house in

Anson. Giles Lollar went blind in his old age, spent his days sitting on the porch, looking out but not seeing. In 1915 Sallie Lollar died, and in 1917 Grandpa Lollar followed. When the house was sold and the estate divided, Myra received a small inheritance of a thousand dollars or so. She used the money to buy the eighty acres of deep shinnery south of the road, just below Fletcher Caffey's place. The heavy post oak thicket provided mountains of stovewood for the home place, and the small field plot was rented for farming each year. When the renter sold his crop and paid Myra her share, the money made a considerable supplement to her egg and butter income.

As time and money would allow, Mart began to improve the two scruffy pieces of land. He had some of the shinnery cleared off and had good fences built on both places. Neither place had dependable water, so Mart wanted better wells on them eventually.

Mr. McKeever lived several miles to the east, in the Funston community, and he witched for water all over south Jones County. Whether by skill or by accident, a good many water wells came to be located over the country in the places located by his divining rod. When he came to the home place one day, Mart set him to work. There was a well on the place already, but the water was hard and bitter, the tank a good ways from the pasture. Mr. McKeever went down toward the barn and began to walk out the country, the forked stick held out front of him, its prongs taut and the "V" pointing skyward. When the tip of the stick suddenly dipped and pointed to the ground, Mr. McKeever marked the spot and went on. When he crossed over the point again, bisecting his original route, the willow stick again reversed and pointed to the ground. Mart staked the point, then arranged for the man to witch on the shinnery place.

The well on the home place never was dug, but water was needed badly on Myra's land. Mart had a hired man living there making improvements and working the farmland, and he put the man to work digging where Mr.

McKeever's rod had indicated. The hired man went to work and in a few days he had moved a good many bucket loads of dirt and had the well down around thirty feet. Water came seeping into the hole, good water and plenty of it.

But the water was in a sand formation and the well pit would not hold its shape. The loose sand slid and shifted and kept the bottom a slushy bog from which no free water could be drawn. What was needed was a cement lining, so that the sand could be held back and a clear pool could form to feed the sucker rod of a windmill. This was clearly a job for a professional, and Mart knew where to find one. He traveled a few miles to the south and hired Groundhog Ryan, long the foremost welldigger in these parts. He lived in the shinnery, near Hawley and not far from the river, in a house built of rock blasted from a dozen wells. Munroe was his given name, though no one ever called him that.

Groundhog Ryan came to Myra's property, built the pit and finished the well. Later Mart had occasion to do business with him again.

The original well on the Truby place was shallow and weak and undependable. Mart knew that there was a good aquifer farther down, and when he was ready to find it, he hired Groundhog Ryan to do the job. Since Ned Welch was living on the place at the time, he helped with the work of deepening the old well.

Groundhog Ryan dug wells by hand, using hand tools and buckets to move earth and tunnel into the ground. He was practically fearless, having no hesitation about lowering himself into any shaft despite various kinds of potential disasters. When he dug the well on the Truby land, Groundhog Ryan hit bedrock after a few days and told Mart that he would be needing some dynamite. Mart brought the sticks from town and gave them to the welldigger. Groundhog took a few of the sticks and lowered himself into the shaft at the end of a rope. As the well digger dropped into the deep pit, the rope was let out from a windlass up top, the crank manned by Ned Welch.

Groundhog Ryan went to work in the bedrock at the bottom, drilled holes and set the charge, laid a long fuse and lit it. "O.K., pull me up outa' here."

Ned Welch was not a big man, but he was eager to get the other man out of the hole and high tail it away from the opening and sizzling fuse. He worked furiously at the crank. Finally the grimy welldigger surfaced and climbed out onto the ground and straightened up. "What was your hurry?" he kidded. The two men headed for the barn, and as Groundhog Ryan put his hand on the door to pull it open, the earth rumbled and the blast sent shattered pieces of rock skyward, causing a shower of fragments around the hole. Groundhog Ryan left the hole alone the rest of that day to let the fumes clear out, then repeated the whole process twice more before the well was finished.

Because of the rent farm bought from her inheritance, Myra was better off than a good many of the farm wives. With the yearly share payment and her egg and butter money, she always had money of her own, and while Mart managed the main sources of income closely and personally, he pretty well left Myra alone with hers. Thus she was able to fulfill many of her own wants for home and family. Myra liked to read and she wanted to encourage reading in the children, so she bought books and kept them out around the house. Myra's money bought many of the boys their first store bought britches and supplied the older girls with dress-up clothes.

For years a regular Saturday ritual was the stop at the ice house in Anson. When the family was in town, Mart would drive by the ice house before heading out for home and buy a block of ice for the weekend. Through the warm months, the family could have iced tea and homemade ice cream for a weekend treat, and by Sunday afternoon the block of ice would be gone. Between meals the chipped and melting block was kept wrapped in towels, sitting in a tub. This arrangement went on for a good long while, until Myra took some of her money and bought an ice box, an upright cabinet in which ice would last and keep perishables good for several days.

Before 1920 hand cranked phonographs began to appear in Jones County. The music machine was a curiosity that quickly caught the fancy of Myra's children whenever they chanced to see one in town or in the home of a neighbor. Before very long, Myra put in an order to the Edison Company, and in a few weeks came a big box with the Edison Phonograph inside.

The music was not on discs, but on grooved cylinders that fit over a spindle. When the crank was turned, energy was stored up in a spring mechanism that would keep the cylinder spinning for several minutes. When the cylinder was set in motion, a needle was lowered onto the grooves, and out came the music. The sound wasn't the best, what with the uneven speed of the spindle and a primitive device for amplification. Nonetheless, the children were fascinated. Over and over again they listened to the talking record of "The Preacher and the Bear," and to the "laugh record." The laugh record began with someone playing a trombone. In the middle of the song, a voice came in laughing. Before long the trombone player was tickled and laughing too, and as the record wore on more and more laughers joined in, both on the record and those listening to it. By the end of the cylinder, the people before the Edison phonograph were holding their sides.

Rudolph took to the phonograph, and especially to the records of good singers like John McCormick and Gene Austin. Time and again Rudolph listened and studied on John McCormick's fine voice ringing out stirring tenor solos. Rudolph aspired to a singing career, and he spent many hours practicing the techniques that he could pick up from the records. A dream born before the old Edison phonograph would later take him to New York and Chicago, to theatres and clubs and fairs.

In the late 1920s one of the Anson merchants was pushing radios. By this time there were stations that would carry into Jones County homes. The man persuaded Mart to put a radio in his house and try it. Mart agreed, and the radio never went back to the shop. The radio came in two parts, the big speaker sitting up on top of the battery case and tuner. There were three dials, and all three had to be synchronized before the station would come in clear. The radio was powered by a dry cell battery and a wet cell battery.

One of the earliest conveniences to find its way into the country houses was the telephone. Phone lines were strung in the Elliott community just before the first world war. On makeshift posts, the line ran in sagging segments from one farmhouse to the next. The M.L. Caffey place got a phone and a phone number —9038F4. The phone was mounted on a wall, with the old style earpiece wired to the box and a crank on the side for ringing other stations.

The Caffeys shared a party line with the neighbors and made calls by giving the right number of rings with the crank. Four turns made four rings in all of the houses on the party line, and meant that the call was for a neighbor. In this case, any of the neighbors might answer until the caller had the intended party on the line. To make a call beyond the party line, the caller gave one ring for the operator at the central office. "This is Central," came the response, and then the caller told the number and was connected with the other party. Whenever the crank was turned to give a ring, the phone jangled in every house on the party line, so that a curious neighbor could pick up and listen in to see what was going on in any call.

About 1915 a new curiosity had begun to appear along the country roads. Mart's children had their first good look at an automobile when Fess Neal came to the house courting one of the girls. His auto was little more than a chassis, tires, radiator, steering column, and engine. There was one double seat, but not the slightest hint of a body.

One day Mart went to town and paid $375 for a new 1917 Model T Ford, the first auto in the Elliott community. He drove it home and kept it under an overhang of the barn, began using it regularly. The buggy became more a second means of transportation, something that the teenaged children might use to get around. Within a few years Mart had traded for a Dodge touring car. Just after World War I came a season when the grain crop was bountiful. The maize stalks were heavy, their tops drooping with the heads of robust grain. Mart brought the crop in and piled the barn full of fresh cut grain. But the maize was green, and on a steamy fall day it burst into flame spontaneously, setting fire to the barn and burning it to the ground, car and all. Mart went to town and bought another car, and thereafter there were new ones at regular intervals—the 1925 Chevy, the 1928 Ford, and so on up to the 1938 Ford.

Light and heating improved only gradually, in small steps that came along several years apart. As long as the old house stood, Myra cooked on a wood stove and heat came from a fireplace and from a wood stove in the girls' room. When the new house was built, a kerosene cook stove was installed in the kitchen and kerosene heaters were placed in other rooms. With these improvements the younger boys no longer had to devote so many hours to wood cutting, but they did have to live with the smell of the coal oil burners. Finally after the children were grown and gone, Myra had a butane tank mounted out back and bought a butane refrigerator to go along with her butane cook stove and room heaters.

From the earliest years Myra liked to read in the evenings. For years she got by on the dim yellow light of a kerosene lamp that burned from a wick and was little better than candlelight. Later came the newer and better "Aladdin" lamps that had mantles instead of wicks. With these the coal oil was pressurized until it came out as a vapor to burn brightly off the net-like mantle. When the mantle was old and burnt out, it turned to ash, crumbled at the slightest touch. It wasn't until the mid 1940s, when Myra was alone on the home place, that electrical lines came to the shinnery. Finally the Rural Electric Co-op did bring brighter lights to the country people. When this happened, Boyd came home and spent several days wiring the house.

133

The buildings on the home place were subject to various kinds of natural and unnatural disasters. What with the unrelenting forces of the West Texas weather and the wear and tear of the large family, they were far from indestructible. All of the structures had to be replaced at one time or another, some of them more than once, over the life of the home place.

One of the first to go was the barn in which the Dodge touring car perished. After its demise in the fire of 1919, two new structures were built to take its place. A new barn was built near the site of the old one, and a separate car shed was built in a more convenient and logical place, out by the road.

The car shed was built for one vehicle, with an overhang added later to house another. The shed served for several years, until Mart's boys finally got the best of it. It eventually came to be in bad shape, and Glenn and Dalton helped make it that way. The old building started having its problems when Dalton backed a car out with the car door open, springing the door and widening the shed in the process. Then Glenn backed out with one of the garage doors not quite open, pulling the door off and leaving it hanging by a hinge. When Glenn finally ran through the back of the shed, its time was clearly finished. It was torn down and piled for scrap. It was a sign of the times that the new shed was built double wide to hold two autos from the start.

Razz Fry built the new barn and it was not what you could call well built. After a few years the supporting uprights, posts sunken into the ground, had about rotted out at ground level. With a pig rooting around at the base of one of the walls, the posts suddenly gave way and the wall dropped down off the rotten nubs, pinning the pig underneath. After a time the plaintive squeals were heard back at the house and Mart and the boys came running to see what could be the matter. They took steel bars and two-by-fours and worked at prying up underneath the wall, finally lifting it enough that the poor humiliated pig could squirm out and trot off to a place of safe retreat.

The walls of the barn could not be left to sit directly on the ground, else the entire building would sooner or later rot out and ruin. Mart and his younger sons, now grown up into their teens, went to the pasture and gathered in some solid oak stumps. These they hauled in and threw down by the barn to be worked up under the old walls.

At this time Boyd carried in the pocket of his bib overalls an old Ingersoll pocket watch. The watch belonged to Viola, and had cost about a dollar. Sometime while the work went on the watch fell from its place in the pocket. Its absence was not discovered until one of the thrown stumps landed squarely on the watch and completely demolished it, leaving only a jillion scattered parts and bits of the broken crystal. When Boyd saw the hopeless wreckage of the watch, he could only think of the smooth, rounded glass that had covered the watch face. "Where is my *trystal?*" he moaned.

Despite the makeshift repairs, the building continued to deteriorate, and by 1936 it was a complete wreck. With Roosevelt's recovery policies beginning to stem the worst of the Depression and put a little money in the pockets of farmers who had survived, Mart now ventured to have a new barn built—one with storage space for feed grain, shelter for animals, and covered storage for the farm implements.

A less expensive but more immediate loss occurred when the old one-holer outhouse bit the dust. The building stood north and west of the house, just beyond the cellar. It served its purpose faultlessly until at last, in the midst of the spring gales, a powerful gust blew it down and tore it asunder. So vital a facility could hardly be spared for very long, so Mart turned in right away to build a new outhouse, this one straight back from the house in the shelter of a windbreak created by the pasture trees.

*   *   *

135

World War I may have made a shambles of Europe, but it brought prosperity to Jones County. Cotton prices went sky high, producing some of the most profitable years ever for the farmers. Then in 1920 prices suddenly fell by half in a precipitous decline known as the "Twenty Break." Many of the farmers met disaster when the new lower prices left them unable to service their mortgages. Several of the neighbors were ruined, but home owners like Mart were able to get by to better times, sustaining little long term damage. Prices recovered some in the early twenties, so when Mart got ready to build a new house, he had the money.

In early 1923 Mart made a trip to the bank in Anson and withdrew enough money to build the house—three or four thousand dollars. It was his intention to begin the work in early summer so that the house could be finihsed in time for cold weather. When Myra took sick for a long spell, he put off starting the project and buried the money at the foot of a peach tree west of the house. By the spring of 1924 Myra was better, so Mart dug up the money and set the work in motion.

When the time came to start the work, everything inside the house was packed up and moved outside. Some of the furniture went to the barn, some to a tent that would be used as a bedroom. A second tent made a makeshift kitchen, and a brush arbor was built to serve as a dining shelter. The sons and daughters slept in a tent or under the stars, according to the evening's weather. Mart and Myra slept in the cellar, and this was not a bad place to sleep; even on the most sultry of summer nights, the cellar stayed cool.

All summer long the work went on, the new house taking shape as the weeks wore on. Mart was not inclined to put out the kind of money that would have been required to hire regular professional carpenters from town. Instead, he hired two old farmers who lived at Truby and did a little carpentry work here and there. Mr. Ball and Mr. Nabors came to do the main job of putting up the frame and walls. They stayed over during the job and slept out on cots. Other neighbors came to do various parts of the work as the summer went on, each one adding some new wrinkle as the house took shape. While the building went on, Mart and the boys did the field work, kept the crops coming along as usual. In all, there was a lot of hubbub around the place, and Myra and Olga were kept stirring in their efforts to feed the family and the workmen from the primitive kitchen.

First the old house was torn down and broken up into piles of scrap, some of which went back into the new house. Then a new foundation was set, this time one anchored in concrete and covered with underpinnings that made the sidewalls appear solid to the ground. The new house was laid out in one big rectangle, three bedrooms along the east side from front to back, with living room, dining room, and kitchen along the west side. A covered front porch faced out toward the road, same as before. The house was built right where the old one had stood, on the high ground of the southwest corner, butted up against the old cistern so that it still served to catch drinking water off the roof.

John Rice was among the neighbors who came to do part of the work on the new house. When the frame was up and secure, he and Boyd spent several days nailing boards across the trusses to deck the roof. In order to get at the upper part of the house, they stood on a board laid across the two-by-fours that served as rafters. The board lapped off over the rafters at either end, so that the two men had to stand on it together, one toward each end, in order to keep it balanced. One morning as Boyd and Mr. Rice were at work on the plank, Boyd stepped off it onto the rafter and the plank flopped up skyward, leaving John Rice to fall through at the other end. As Mr. Rice fell, his pantleg caught on a nail, turning him upside down and sending him hurtling head first. The nail ripped through the pantleg and John Rice tumbled headlong into the space in the floor joist, between the beams where the floor planks would be laid. Mr. Rice emerged scratched and battered, but no bones were broken. As always, he took the mishap in good humor. As he pushed up out of the joist and turned himself upright again, he looked up at Boyd to say, "Well . . . I taken another high dive."

When the house was about finished and the shingles were on, Vincent Penticost was hired to paint. Since Rudolph was home from school for the summer, he was assigned to help with the painting. Rudolph was now twenty years old, Vincent a few years older. Vincent had done his time in the country schools, but his was not a family of scholars, so after his school years Vincent had just gone to work in the home country, farming and doing odd jobs.

When it came time to paint the roof, Vincent and Rudolph took buckets of black paint and climbed a ladder set against the east side of the house. Braced against the slant roof, they worked across the broad sections of roof surface, stroking the paint into the raw shingles. When Rudolph had used the last of his paint, he climbed back down off the roof for a drink of water and a fresh bucket. He started back up the ladder and was approaching the edge of the roof when a misstep threw the ladder off balance and sent it crashing sideways to the ground. Rudolph grabbed onto the eave by arms and elbows, held there for dear life. With the full paint bucket dropping in mid-air and no one near it, he hollered out, "Catch that bucket!" No one could or would have caught the bucket, and it hit the ground and spattered a great eruption of paint all over the ground and the lower wall of the house. Mart was standing near the cistern, just observing as the work went along. He came on a run to where Rudolph was dangling off the side of the house. Mart grasped him around the waist, helped him safely to the ground.

When Rudolph had regrouped, he took a fresh bucket of paint, re-set the ladder, and crawled up on the house to take his place painting. For the rest of the morning, Vincent Penticost kept on painting his way across the roof. When by chance the calamity recurred in his mind, he would throw his head back and burst out in a big laugh all over again. Rudolph kept his head down in his work, kept on swishing the paint brush, stewed in a slow burn. He never saw anything laughable in the incident.

*   *   *

The very next summer after the house was built, Mart took a notion to take the family and make a trip to visit the old Mississippi home. Visits back had been few. Mart had only been the one time, when his mother had died in 1906. Myra, always occupied with babies or small children, had not been back at all. By now Mart and Myra had been gone from the old country for thirty-five years. Many of the home folks had surely died, others would be well along in years. With all of the kids now big enough to see after themselves and with conditions generally prosperous, it seemed a likely time to make such a trip if it was ever to happen at all. Glenn was now about eleven years old, Dalton thirteen, Boyd seventeen.

Mart had a new 1925 Chevrolet in which to make the trip. Over the several years of its manufacture, the model had earned an uncomplimentary nickname. It came to be called the ''490 Chevy''—four days on the road and ninety days in the garage. In mid-July, a few days before departure, he went to the bank in Anson and drew out two one-hundred dollar gold certificates.

Wiley and Rudolph were grown and home from college, and they were left to run the farm for the three weeks that the others would be away. Mart and Myra took the three younger boys and started out toward Fort Worth and beyond.

The drive to northern Mississippi took time and patience, what with the early day auto and the miles of crooked gravel roads. The ride was hot and dusty, the days of driving long. The family rode over the bumps and byways all day long, Boyd doing the driving and Mart giving advice as he saw fit. At evening they stopped to camp along

139

the way. They camped at a park near Dallas, by the roadside at Marshall, Texas; and again part way across Louisiana.

The 490 Chevy made its way across Louisiana and crossed the Mississippi on a ferry—a great wide barge with room for several cars. The ferry had two levels, cars on the first level down below and a scenic deck for passengers above.

When the ferry landed a few miles below Vicksburg, the landing broke sharply upward, leaving the autos to climb a steep embankment to where the road leveled out. The Chevy labored mightily at the incline, so much so that Myra was alarmed, doubtful that the car could make it up the hill. When the car rolled back to make another run at it, she opened the door and climbed down onto the roadway, determined to walk up the incline instead of riding. Boyd wasn't altogether certain that the Chevy would manage the grade either, but he put it in low and gave it gas, and the car rumbled right on up and over the top.

At Jackson, Mississippi, smoke billowed from under the floorboard and swirled around Boyd's feet. In a scramble the car was emptied of its passengers, all of them baffled and alarmed at the black smoke. Mart pulled up the floorboard to find the battery afire. The boys scooped up dirt to throw on the flames, and finally Mart put his hand to the battery and swept the fire off it. It was with this experience that Mart learned to keep the headlights on during the day on long journeys, lest the generator overcharge and cause the battery to go haywire.

The fire in Jackson caused a day's delay. By the time the car was out of the garage and on the road north, it was too late to reach the home country by nightfall. The auto rolled toward the old hills through towering stands of oak and pine, pulled into Tupelo at dusk. Seeing no good place to camp, Mart finally pulled to the side of the street to ask after a suitable place. He hailed a respectable looking man, told where he was from and where the family was going, asked whether there might be a park in the area.

There wasn't, but the man was cordial. "My front yard's just as good as any," he offered, motioning toward a fine grassy lawn leading up toward a big antebellum mansion. Mart was grateful for the invitation, pulled in off the street and put down stakes for the night.

The lawn fell away from the house in a long slope that had been terraced, so that there were level strips winding evenly across the lawn with gentle slopes in between. The boys pitched their sleeping pallets along one of the level strips and went to bed. Sometime in the night Boyd rolled off the ledge and off his pallet into the wet grass and took a bad cold.

The first stop in the old home country was to be the home of Sandy Lollar, Myra's uncle. Uncle Sandy lived at Baldwyn, just over the line into Prentiss County, a short drive from Tupelo. As the Chevy came into the outskirts of the little town of Baldwyn, Mart motioned toward a house and had Boyd pull over in front of it. Mart got out and walked up to knock at the door. In the car, the boys were puzzled. "Mama, is this Uncle Sandy's house?" one of them asked. "Well, no, I don't think so."

Mart knocked and a woman opened the door. Mart told who he was and what the family was doing and where they were going. They had been on the road almost a week, he explained, and the kids were awfully dirty for making an appearance at their kinfolks' house. Mart wanted to know whether they might come inside and take a bath. The woman agreed and Mart walked back to have the boys bring the suitcases and come along inside. They bathed and scrubbed in the woman's house, packed up and went on their way to Uncle Sandy Lollar's house.

A few days were spent in Baldwyn with the Lollars, and then the Chevy was pointed north toward the old hills south of Booneville. The auto rolled through town and into the hills toward the Bennett place. After the years of hearing how Abb Bennett had said such and such or how Abb Bennett had done thus and so, the boys were finally to meet the man. The Chevy wound its way among the country lanes, and finally came upon Abb Bennett at the Meadow Creek Cemetery. Abb made the old friends welcome, looked the young boys over, showed them all up to the clearing where his big white house stood.

For three days Abb went all over the old home country with Mart and Myra and the boys. They went to Myra's old home, to the cabin where Mart had grown up, to the church at Shady Grove, and up a long hollow to where the Hill family lived.

Sometime each day Mart and Abb took the boys, Mart's three and Abb's two, and went to Bennett Lake, a reservoir that Abb had built on his land by putting an earthen dam across the headwaters of Doniphan Creek. While the boys played in the water, Mart and Abb would lean up against the trunk of a stout old shade tree and talk.

Glenn, now ten years old, wasn't yet a swimmer. While the older boys splashed and swam out in the lake, Glenn played in the shallow part near the edge. One morning Abb took a notion to teach Glenn how to swim and called him over to where he stood. Between Glenn and Abb Bennett was an inlet creek that ran into Bennett Lake. Rather than make the long walk around to where the creek narrowed and he could step across, Glenn just waded out across it, expecting that it would be shallow. Glenn walked straight off into the deeper channel and went down like a rock. Abb Bennett, though crippled to a slight limp from two near catastrophic accidents, came up like a scared rabbit. In a few long strides he hit the water and took hold of Glenn, who was fighting and sputtering to stay up. Abb brought him safely to shore.

Later on, Myra and Mrs. Bennett wanted to know what had brought Abb home all soaked on a perfectly sunny day. Abb made up some story about wanting to swim when there were ladies present at the lake that day, so he had left his clothes on, but of course that story didn't fly, and it came out that Glenn had almost drowned in Bennett Lake. Myra was understandably upset and she didn't want Glenn going back in Bennett Lake, but he did anyway.

142

For three or four nights the Caffeys stayed in the white farmhouse with Abb and Alma and the Bennett kids. Each night Mart and Abb sat up in the kitchen long after the others had turned in. Together they recalled boyhood days and caught up on the intervening years—thirty-five of them.

As much as Mart and Myra enjoyed seeing the old places and people, it wasn't home anymore. After all the years on the Texas prairie, Myra had grown accustomed to the wide, far flung spaces, to the big sky and the land that lay flat so that a person could see across it. When she came in to breakfast at the Bennett house, she would speak of how the great high oaks seemed to smother her.

When all of the visiting was done, the 490 Chevy left the old country, rumbled across northern Mississippi and crossed over into Arkansas. The engine had begun to lose power, and now it was laboring mightily to clear the slightest hills. At Hot Springs it gave out. In two days layover time, the engine was completely overhauled.

With the car whole again, the family rumbled over miles of Arkansas hills and into the tall pine country of east Texas. In another day they were back through Fort Worth and onto the familiar home prairie. They covered the last dusty miles through Mineral Wells and Albany and Anson, rolled down the country lane to the cotton rows and shinnery breaks of the home place. When Mart pulled the Chevy up before the car shed by his house, he still had one of the gold certificates in his billfold.

*   *   *

Mart wasn't especially looking to buy land. He just happened to hear of a deal that sounded awfully good, and the more he thought about it, the more he was inclined to go and have a look. The land was in Dawson County—good farmland in the kinds of expansive, open tracts that were beginning to pay off big on the high plains. In the old ranching country of the Texas Panhandle and on the plains stretching southward, much of the old range had been turned over to farmers. Now taking shape was the kind of larger scale farm to which would belong the future. Though most of Mart's kids were by now grown and into other vocational pursuits, the three younger boys were still at home. Moreover, Mart still had the striving edge that set him mulling and figuring whenever a promising trade possibility could be detected on the horizon. With a larger spread on the land to the west, Mart might make big money in his last working years and then leave a top notch farming enterprise to be carried on by one or two sons.

Mart and his nephew Tom Caffey occasionally went in on business deals, and now they went together to look at the Dawson County land. They made the trip out west to Lamesa and looked up the agent handling the land. From a farming standpoint, the land was beautiful—flat as a table top and not a tree on it. All across Dawson County, farmers were finding the land just right for cotton. The soil was potent, and yearly it produced some of the highest cotton yields anywhere in the state. Mart liked the looks of it all, and at day's end he put down earnest money on a section of land. Over the miles back home to Jones County, Mart and Tom considered the ins and outs of the country they had seen, the irrevocable risk of pulling up from established roots in Jones County to make such a move. Mart had a few weeks in which to make up his mind and follow up on his option or let it go. He was coming off some moderately good crop years and he had quite a bit of money on hand, but he would still have to lean on the bank for a loan and sign a promissory note if he were to have the land.

In the end, Mart decided against the move and let the chance pass. He forfeited his earnest money. Tom had pretty much decided that the land wasn't worth the asking price, at least not to him. Mart was reluctant to uproot home and family and make a new start entirely on his own, and he didn't much care for the idea of taking on a big mortgage. In backing away from the deal, Mart also back-ed away from the lingering idea of a bold move to one more piece of new country and one more prospect of building and improving a piece of land until it gave up greater satisfaction and prosperity. Mart didn't go looking any more.

While Mart was busy accumulating shinnerylands and cattle and hogs and chickens and automobiles and children, he had also been accumulating years. By 1927 Mart was pushing fifty-eight, and he was long since set in the ways and paths established over his thirty-five years in Jones County. No longer did he feel inclined to respond to the impulse that once had set him striking out for the In-dian Territory, impatient with his circumstances and confi-dent in a bright future. Steel rails and wagon wheels no longer made him think of the good life that might be waiting across a stretch of unseen prairie. Mart went about his business around the home place and left the chasing of new country to younger men.

*   *   *

Mart did finally get a tractor up in the 1930s. When he did so, it wasn't so much out of an impulse to have the latest innovation, but simply as a practical solution to months of frustration in trying to match up a working team of mules. Among the old time farmers of south Jones County, there was a good deal of hesitancy about switching over from mules and horses to tractors. Many of the men scoffed at the idea of tractors, certain that they would stall in the deep sand beds of the shinneylands. But Mart final-ly gathered up his old work animals and implements, threw in a note receivable from one of the neighbor farmers and a hundred dollars cash, and took delivery on a gasoline powered Farmall tractor. When it came time to turn the land, the tractor ground its way all around Mart's field with no great effort, even in the deep sands of the northeast corner.

9. Schoolhouse Days

After the rows of cotton plants were chopped clean of weeds each summer, Mart still had a month or more in which to busy his children before the school term began. Beginning toward the end of August and lasting through September, the boys were sent with a wagon and team to cut stovewood on the eighty acre shinnery tract that Myra had purchased. The wood cutting continued until cotton bolls began to come ripe for picking, and then the boys were set to work in the field dragging cotton sacks up and down the rows. By the time the fifteenth of October rolled around, the prospect of five months in Elliott Schoolhouse had begun to look pretty good.

Come mid-autumn each year, the children put away their cotton sacks and took up school books. Daily they walked the half mile to Elliott Schoolhouse, just down and across the road from the house, or the longer distance to Pleasant Hill School, two miles to the north. Some of the boys went as far as Truby when the closer schools discontinued the middle grades, and the three younger boys went on to the high school in Anson as well.

With their primitive materials, ill prepared and transient teachers, and the hodgepodge of grade levels lumped together, there is no doubt that the country schools left much to be desired in instructional quality. There were things that Mart's children learned at home, though, that helped to overcome the schools' deficiencies. At home Mart made certain that his children learned about truth and honesty, and they learned how to work. Altogether, the children reached the end of their time in the country schools with enough learning and enough grit that any one of them with the inclination could succeed in college, as most of them did.

By the time Mart's family was settled on the home place, there were dozens of little schools scattered over Jones County—at Tuxedo, at Oak Grove, Nienda, Anderson Chapel, Pleasant Valley, and many of the other rural communities. The one and two room schools were administered by "common school districts," in which trustees from the local community took care of the school's business under the general direction of the county commissioners' court or the county superintendent. The rural schools came to be spaced perhaps two to four or five miles apart, so that each served a relatively small number of pupils.

The country schools were products of a pattern of settlement that found people spread somewhat evenly over the open countryside, large families working small farms. The few towns were large enough only to provide support enterprises for the outlying farmers, whose production made up the sole economic sustenance of the region. In these days, it would have been no great trick to scour a few square miles of Jones County and come up with fifty or sixty children off a dozen farms. Moreover, there was no such thing as school transportation, so the school had to be within practical walking distance of its pupils.

Even before public schools were organized, many of the communities had started their own schools paid for by local subscription. In 1884 the county commissioners established the first twelve public school districts, and from there the number grew. By 1915, when the home place was at its peak in population—the youngest child born and the oldest not yet gone—the rural school system was also at its peak in Jones County. At this time there were more than sixty common school districts in the county. Already in the making, though largely unnoticed, were changes that would one day bring about a steady succession of consolidation moves, so that eventually fewer than a dozen schools would be left. In time the hulks of vacant

country schools would stand across the prairie with abandoned windmills and a few dilapidated old farmhouses as
almost the only visible reminders that—yes, this country
did have a past. But for the time being, pupils growing up
across Jones County experienced their school days in a setting that their own children would only imagine.

When it came to education, Mart and Edgar didn't
see eye to eye. Each had his own point of view, and in each
family the consequences could be seen years later as the
children of each brother went into their own vocations.
Both Mart and Edgar had been taught by their preacher
father that honesty was number one, but they came to
have opposite ideas about how this applied to the business
of education. Uppermost in Edgar's mind were his experiences with men who were well educated, but who used
their learning to deceive and take advantage. Edgar came
to conclude that education did more harm than good, that
it provided a temptation and a means toward crookedness.
Accordingly, Edgar never put much emphasis on schooling
for his own kids. If they made it to school for a fair part of
the term, fine; if not, it was nothing to worry over.

Mart thought that his children needed to be
educated. He saw the good and the uses of education,
rather than the few abuses. Mart wasn't blind to the
changes he saw in Abilene and Fort Worth, and in the
rural country of Jones County. Mart's one farm did not offer much promise toward lifetime prosperity for the six
boys, and cheap frontier land was all but gone. There
would be no more moves to new country for his kids or
anyone else's. Instead, the new country of the twentieth
century was in places like Fort Worth and Dallas and
Abilene—places where commerce and the professions now
held out the kinds of opportunity that the new lands had
once offered. Education would provide the wherewithal for
Mart's children to get out of the home country and make a
good life somewhere else. Mart was thus determined to see
the school years count for something, and this became one
of the lasting aims to which he committed his efforts.

Neighbors might hold their children out of school until the cotton crop was in, but Mart never did. Mexicans could pick the cotton; the kids would stay in school. There was no state law mandating compulsory attendance at the country schools, but Mart's rule did.

Directly across the road from the home place was the farm of the Elliott family. In 1902, Mr. Elliott sold the county a corner lot off the east end of his land, and the first Elliott Schoolhouse was built. It wasn't much to look at. It was a one room box, the outside walls built of plain, unpainted lumber, boxed and stripped in the simplest fashion. Inside were plain desks with two-seat benches, and at the front was a chalkboard. A cast iron stove radiated scant heat from the center of the room outward toward the drafty, uninsulated board walls. The schoolhouse sat near the intersection of two country lanes, in a rough schoolyard cleared from out of the surrounding brush.

When a teacher was hired for one of the country schools, it was for the term. After school let out, the teacher generally moved on, and several months later the trustee began again to find a new teacher and arrange for the coming term. Occasionally a teacher might stay two or even three years, but more often, it was one year, then a new teacher the next. The pay was pitifully low, which was why Mart was not very interested in continuing after teaching the one term at Pleasant Hill to tide him over during his first year in Jones County. When Elliott Schoolhouse opened in 1902, the first teacher was paid a better-than-average salary of fifty-five dollars a month.

Elliott Schoolhouse generally had one teacher, as did many of the other country schools. When there was more than one teacher, the one working with the upper grades was designated the "Head Teacher." With no principal or state hierarchy overseeing things and without the more regimented organization of a larger school, there was a good deal of independence in the individual school. What went on was determined pretty much by the character and inclinations of the teacher and pupils, tempered somewhat by the sensibilities of the community. So it was that the country schools saw their share of errant pupils and unorthodox teachers, each limited not so much by systems or policies as by what he could pull off in a given situation.

The teacher often was strictly on his own with no one to intervene or back up his actions. This could work to his advantage or not, depending on his own qualities and strengths and those of the pupils. Despite the usual advantage in age, the teacher didn't always come out on top in conflicts, as when cousin Haskell was in school at Pleasant Hill in 1905. The main problem that the teacher had to contend with there was that of having three of the Burdine boys in the one classroom. On one side, near the window, was Jess. Toward the front sat Ed Burdine. Haskell, eleven years old, shared a desk with Ernest, who was older and bigger and took up more than his share of the bench. The trouble began one morning when Ernest shoved Haskell off the end of the bench. One thing led to another, and before long it was clear that unruliness was to be the main business of the day.

Ed Burdine was only thirteen, but he was big for his age, and mean. He went picking at some of the pupils around him, escalating his devilishness as he saw the teacher's annoyance level rise. The teacher rebuked Ed and went on with the lessons, calling each grade to the front in turn for their daily recitations. Ed went on bothering first one pupil and then another, paying no mind at all to the teacher or to his own lessons. Finally the teacher rose from his place and snatched from the corner a fat stick of about two feet long. With the vehemence of his pent up irritation, he began to thrash at Ed Burdine. The boy would not be subdued. He stood from his bench, pulled the stick away, and broke it in two. Ernest stood and stepped into one aisle, Jess in another. Seeing what he was up against, the teacher stepped back out of Ed's reach and told the boy that he'd better take his books and get on home. Ed left, the brothers sat back down, and the lessons went on.

In a few days Mr. Burdine came to the schoolhouse and arranged for Ed to come back.

It was a ragtag collection of children that showed up at the schoolhouse each fall when the term began. All in the one plain schoolroom were gangly boys approaching manhood and towheaded boys running barefoot, little girls clinging to older siblings and bigger girls toughened to shinnery life. Clothes were plain, many of them stitched from flour sacks or inexpensive cotton cloth. There were dresses and hair ribbons and overalls and flop hats, all in varying shapes and sizes.

Mart's children took a lunch from home each morning when they trudged off toward Elliott Schoolhouse or Pleasant Hill. The contents of the lunch pails were not always to their liking. Whenever the children complained about what their mother packed for them, Mart would launch into a tale of his own school days back in Mississippi. In those days, as now, pupils had scattered to their customary spots in the schoolyard when noontime came around. Mart liked to tell of two boys he remembered, who repaired to their place under a big shade tree each day to share their poverty. The boys were from one of the poorest of the poor families around Shady Grove, and their lunch was the same day after day—a bucket of cold blackeyed peas. Together the boys took handfulls from the pail and munched them down. Though others had more and better, the boys carried no bitterness. One noon hour as they ate, Mart heard one boy turn to his brother to remark, "Bill, ain't peas good?"

In keeping order and meting out justice for minor offenses, the teacher had plenty of leeway. Plain, old-fashioned thrashings were not uncommon, but some of the teachers were more original. One woman teacher at Elliott had more authority than common sense. She demonstrated that one day by making Lela Mae Dyer drink down twelve cups of water as punishment for some small infraction. This penalty made the girl sick and won the teacher the contempt of her pupils for the rest of the term.

One year there was an unusual amount of rowdiness around the Elliott community. Some of the older boys had fallen into a habit of issuing challenges and calling bluffs and fighting for no good reason other than to prove who was the toughest. There was nothing criminal about the ruckus, but it needed to be curbed before it could get out of hand. The boys who were involved were not essentially mean or bad, but they sometimes needed someone to keep them in line.

At this time Mart was the trustee for the Elliott school. He stewed around about the problem for a time and felt obligated to do something about the ruffians and their ever more frequent melees. As the new school term approached, it occurred to Mart that what was needed was a teacher who could set the bully boys right back down on their own terms. Mart needed a teacher who had come up the hard way himself, who could deal with the roughhousing immediately and directly. Mart heard of a man in the next county who might be suitable. When he drove over to meet the teacher, Mart returned satisfied that this was the strong influence that the Elliott boys needed. The man was hired.

Come the next fall, things settled down some. The new teacher did in fact inspire restraint, and the former rowdies walked lightly when he was around. Mart might have been ready to savor his own cleverness, had not the solution suddenly soured. Halfway through the school term, the teacher's rough cut brother came into the community to live with him, and the combination brought out the worst in both of them. The new arrival was inclined to talk big, drink too much, and anger quickly. He soon became an abrasive influence to most all of the neighbors, and together the brothers began to ignite minor scrapes. The teacher and his brother became the new problem.

When the school year ended, it was plainly understood that the teacher was not to be hired for another term. All that remained for Mart was to settle up for the school district and let the men be on their way. It was for this purpose that Mart drove east on the road one morning. He pulled off the road and stopped before a plain, two room house between the John Rice place and Fletcher's. Mart was admitted to the house, and in the conversation that followed, the two brothers began to make claims and demands beyond what Mart had months before agreed to pay. The men went into their bullying way of talking and pushed their bluff hard. Mart refused the new demands; he wouldn't budge. He paid only what the school owed. Hard words were exchanged and Mart backed out of the room and off the porch and went home. The teacher vowed to pursue the issue tomorrow.

Sometime before daylight broke over the shinnery, Fletcher Caffey took down his shotgun, shoved a handful of shells in a coat pocket, and struck out up the road toward his brother's house. Mart had told him about the trouble, and Fletcher was glad to help. Mart and Fletcher had their coffee and waited inside the house, and in time an auto rumbled along up the road carrying the two ornery brothers. With their belongings piled up in the back seat, the men came to a spot in front of Mart Caffey's house to take care of one item of unfinished business.

Fletcher took his shotgun in hand and walked out the front door and angled across the yard, swinging a leg over the low yard fence and taking it in stride. He crossed the road in front of the car and stood by the far ditch to observe the conversation that would follow. Mart walked to the car and greeted the visitors. The teacher, whose demeanor had been so blustery of late, now was strangely reticent. He mumbled his apology for any misunderstanding, and drove away toward the cane patch and away out of the Elliott country for good.

After the long winter shut up inside the schoolroom, the boys found the warm spring days particularly enticing. At least once a year they could be counted on to play hookey for the day. The Caffey boys took part in these annual celebrations of springtime and youthful rebellion, despite consequences they knew were likely to result. In his way, Mart understood and could even enjoy and appreciate his boys' shenanigans, but he never tolerated them nonetheless. Skipping school meant a whipping if Mart came to learn about it, as he usually did. Some years the boys played their stunt on April Fool's Day. Arriving at the schoolhouse early, they stacked the desks and took off to the river for a day of swimming and picnicking.

On one inviting spring day, the boys at Elliott Schoolhouse happened to hear of a baseball game to be played at Pleasant Hill, just away and over a gentle rise to the north. Among those who thought the game sounded more interesting than the day's lessons were Wiley and Rudolph Caffey and Menco Rice. The boys considered the matter briefly, then abandoned the schoolhouse for the dusty road to Pleasant Hill.

The road to be traveled ran north along the east fence row of the Caffey place. Between the fence row and the house was a half mile of open field, so that one with a keen eye might stand at the house and recognize the familiar silhouettes of family members working at the far end of the field. This being the case, Wiley and Rudolph thought it best to devise some ruse to forestall their father's suspicions, should he happen to look up and notice three figures moving along the road at the far end of his field. The boys walked into a nearby patch and pulled cornstalks. They pulled the leaves off and cut the bare stalks to size, then propped them over their shoulders in imitation of hunters they had seen out walking over the country with their guns at bird season. Mart could be seen far to the west, working at some chore up around the house. The boys made their way along the road, and soon they passed behind the protective barrier of the wooded pasture. From here on, there was no danger of being detected. The boys threw down their cornstalks and frolicked on toward Pleasant Hill.

As they walked they talked of things curious to young boys. The talk turned to swimming, which was something that all of them had done from time to time down on the

Clear Fork. Menco began telling his companions about a fancy way of diving, and soon he was carried away in his enthusiasm. Menco proceeded to demonstrate. He crouched and sprang into the air, flipped head over heels and came down on his head, knocked fully unconscious. When Menco was revived the other boys helped him up, and the three continued on their way past Dixon's field and over onto Pleasant Hill, where the schoolhouse stood not far off.

As the walkers approached the schoolyard, an auto turned the corner and puttered up the road behind them. Mart pulled alongside and let out a big laugh. "You boys have a good time," he said, talking to Wiley and Rudolph, "and I'll see you this evening." With that Mart drove on his way and Wiley and Rudolph crossed over to the schoolyard where the ball game was starting, more somber now in anticipation of the licking that would be waiting for them at home.

Dalton was a long time learning to read. Although he had gone to Elliott school for three years already, he was ten years old before he ever really began to learn. The teachers he had in school either wouldn't teach reading or didn't know how. Dalton had little to show for those first three years of going through the motions of schooling. The one-room teachers, even under the best conditions, were hard pressed to teach a variety of subjects, each on several grade levels, and it was an almost impossible task for them to succeed with every pupil on every subject. The teaching of reading was especially time consuming. It was often allowed to slide in classrooms where three dozen pupils of all ages would have to be kept occupied with lessons while the teacher heard two or three of the little ones read. When Dalton did take a notion to improve his reading, he did so on his own determination. Neither the inspiration nor the know-how came from the school.

In Dalton's tenth summer, Olga finished her school year in Haskell County and came home bringing along a friend, Pauline Anderson. Miss Anderson had with her several books of interest to young boys, and she entertained Dalton and Glenn with stories read aloud from the books. Dalton and Glenn hung on each word as Miss Anderson read the story of "Miss Minerva and William Greenhill." In their own old front room they vicariously experienced the ever more intriguing adventures of *Penrod* and *Huckleberry Finn* as Miss Anderson read a chapter or two at a time. Miss Anderson was a good reader. She didn't just say the words. She spoke in low and mysterious tones of the midnight procession to dig up Peter Wilks, inspired panicky fear when she read about Huck Finn's desperate run from the graveyard. Miss Anderson's voice could produce so many different moods and surprises.

Dalton was annoyed when a meal or bedtime interrupted the story, impatient when Miss Anderson was off somewhere with Olga. Between story times Dalton eyed the book where it lay, frustrated that it would give up none of its adventures without Miss Anderson there to read the words. When Miss Anderson left, there were no more stories. On the day of her departure, Dalton decided that he needed to read better. With Myra's help in making out new words, Dalton began to work his own way through the books he could find around the house. When Dalton returned to Elliott Schoolhouse several months later, he was able to read with anyone his age, and better than a good many who were older.

Elliott Schoolhouse wasn't just for lessons and recitations. It served as a place for occasional social and spiritual events as well. Most notable among these were the school plays to which families and community residents were invited and the Holiness meetings that were sometimes held at the schoolhouse.

The plays presented by the Elliott pupils were of a kind that would be remembered—not so much for dramatic excellence, which they lacked, but rather for unrehearsed surprises, which they had plenty of. Besides the awkward bobbles that typically punctuated performances, there was good humor in the quaint, archaic language spoken by characters in many of the scripts. Among the more memorable productions was "Mrs. Stubbens' Book Agent," which the pupils put on in about 1911. Long years after Elliott Schoolhouse had ceased to exist, Wiley continued to quote the line of an inflated and overly officious door-to-door book salesman. In the play, the line was rendered by the salesman as he finished his call in a client's living room and rose to take his leave: "It is with great reluctance and deep regret that I leave your charming society, but the onerous duties of my profession call me hence."

In the same play, John Caffey played the head of a fairly well-to-do household. As host to the local deacon visiting in his home, John was to issue a gracious invitation for the pastor to step into a pleasant garden patio imagined to be behind the doors of the parlor. When the time came, John mindlessly delivered the words he had memorized: "Garden, come into my deacon."

In later years Dalton went to Elliott Schoolhouse to a teacher he could never quite warm up to. Dalton would occasionally try the teacher's patience with petty mischief, and the two came to regard one another at a distance. When a play was planned and parts were assigned, there was none for Dalton. As the day of the performance approached, Miss Whitley felt pangs of regret to having left three or four of the boys out entirely, and she gave them duties helping with the production in various ways. She enlisted Dalton and a classmate as stage helpers and gave them the responsibility of standing one on either side of the makeshift stage and drawing back the two wagon sheets that were to be rigged as curtains.

On the evening of the performance, all was bedlam. Children darted in every direction while mothers fussed around combing heads and straightening collars and stuffing shirttails. Someone's dog was loose on the stage, and homely looking props were being knocked over as fast as they could be stood back up. Miss Whitley compounded the confusion with her every effort to bring order and get the performance underway. At the height of the chaos, Dalton and the neighbor boy drew the curtain to the delight of a good humored audience and the horrified embarrassment of the teacher. The boys met around back of the school and walked the road home. Dalton had never liked that teacher anyway.

Even more dramatic than the plays were the Holiness church meetings that were held periodically on the school grounds. Here there was fiery preaching and the free flow of wailing and jubilant praise. Between preaching sessions some of the devout brethren lay out in the brush, deeply absorbed in prayer. When preaching went on inside the schoolhouse, the preacher's loud admonishments were often answered with shouts of "Praise the Lord, Glory Hallelujah."

One spring some of the neighbors were promoting the idea of a singing school to be held at the schoolhouse in early April. The Elliott community was none too big to be taking on such an endeavor, so its success was not to be taken for granted. Still, the community seemed to be coming together behind the idea. The instigators talked it up, found most of the neighbors receptive, went ahead with plans and made arrangements for a singing teacher to come for the week and lead the school. Yet to be accomplished was final approval by the school trustees. When the time drew near, the trustees called a community meeting to hear discussion and vote final approval. It was agreed among the three trustees that a vote in opposition by any one of the three would render the singing school idea dead.

On the appointed evening families drove from the outlying farms, gathered at the schoolhouse and packed themselves into the small building, all chairs filled and people standing all around the sides of the room. At the front of the room, the three trustees sat behind a table to preside over the gathering. The meeting began, and proponents of the singing school laid their plans before the community people, found general acceptance as they went along.

At the back of the room, the young school teacher stood against the door frame, her reservations mounting as the discussion wore on. Finally Miss Puckett rustled past the row of men standing against the side aisle and made her way to the front of the room. While some good man said his piece from the audience, she buzzed at the ear of John Rice, a school trustee. The teacher worried that seven evenings of singing school would get the school children home late each night, cause lessons to go neglected, and throw the school into a general uproar for the week.

When the matter had been thrashed over and the community seemed in general agreement about going ahead with the singing school, the chairman called the question to an obligatory vote. "If there is no objection," he announced, "the singing school will commence on the first Sunday in April." He looked to one trustee, then the other. After a dignified pause, John Rice rose from his chair, impossibly and unaccountably. In his casual, hemming and hawing, backgrounding manner, he delivered the knockout blow: "I believe I'll object."

The assembled community sat dumfounded and stunned, silent and disbelieving. With the roomful of people hanging in the uneasy limbo of awkward silence, Wiley Caffey broke the long moment, clearing his throat loudly and self-consciously. This brought first a sprinkling of snickers, then the general laughter into which the meeting dissolved and dispersed.

Dalton and Glenn were among the last pupils to know the days of Elliott Schoolhouse. Even by their time, the middle grades were no longer taught there, so that the older pupils of the Elliott community had to travel the longer distance to Truby for the seventh and eighth grades. Elliott Schoolhouse closed its doors forever in 1931, when the school was consolidated with Pleasant Hill. The building was razed within a few years. Pleasant Hill lasted until 1947 before consolidating with the Anson schools. Truby School stayed open until 1953. The consolidation trend swept over Jones County, the product of irresistible forces. With the quarter section farms no longer feasible, there were fewer families on the land. Families were smaller. Eventually school buses would come to carry the rural pupils to town each day. Time swept over the one and two room schools, leaving them in the wake of a society bent on mobility, bigness, and efficiency.

State boards of education of later days would have been aghast at conditions that prevailed in the country schools—the short terms, low or non-existent standards of teacher preparation, permissive attitudes toward attendance. Somehow, though, the schools delivered a fair helping of readin', writin', and arithmetic, and Mart's children each took on a determination to achieve—one that came from within. All in all, the kids came out of their school days prepared to make it in college and steer toward more promising careers in a time when cheap land was gone and prospects for the small farmer were not good.

10. The Road From Home

When Olga packed up and went off to Stamford College in 1915, there began a steady and irreversible trickle of departures from the home place. Over the next twenty years, one after another of the sons and daughters grew up and away from the family farmstead until only Mart and Myra were left. As Mart's family dispersed, so too did the Rices, the Elliotts, the Dixons, the McLarens, and the other large families that lived on farms for miles around. When these were gone, there were none to replace them. Days were numbered for the country schools and churches, the singing classes and sandlot ball games. It wasn't just a family breaking up during these years, but a way of life.

It was not all that easy to break away from Mart's dominance and go one's own way. Bossiness was deeply engrained in Mart's nature, especially where his children were concerned. He was accustomed to telling them what to do from infancy, and this was a habit that he did not surrender easily. It was in his nature to hold on as long as he could, to have his way as long as any one of the children would let him. Thus when it came time for a parting of the ways, the occasion was not always smooth or pleasant.

It is sometimes said that the older children in a family are treated more severely than the ones who come along after them, and this seems to have been true in Mart's family. It is certainly true that Olga, for all her good hearted nature and hard working ways, did not have a very easy life. All through her early years she caught the brunt of Mart's harshness. In later years she took care of Myra, and absorbed her mother's minor scoldings without complaint.

Olga was the firstborn among all of the children. She

was also the oldest girl, and this particular fact had special importance, at least for Mart. In backwoods Mississippi, it had been customary among some of the families that the oldest daughter was expected to care for her parents in their old age, to remain free from other obligations so that this could be one of her primary purposes in life. Mart subscribed to this peculiar notion, and accordingly, he kept a watchful eye on Olga during her early years. Mart was careful about the young men he would allow to get near any of his girls, but with Olga he was more than just particular. Olga had her courting times, but whenever a young man appeared to have the interest and the necessary qualities to make a likely suitor, Mart seemed all the more intent on running him off. Whenever Mart turned contrary there was no changing his mind. Olga never learned how to successfully counter this streak in her father, nor did she ever make the complete break that might have made her free at the expense of her family ties. She never married.

At one time Olga hoped to become a nurse. She wrote letters to hospitals and nursing schools and received papers telling about the life and work of a nurse, and about nurses' training. When Mart learned of her aspirations, he was adamant; Olga would not be a nurse. Olga kept her hopes for a time, hid the literature beneath her mattress in the girls' room. Bonnie found the papers and grew interested as she read, more interested as she and Olga talked together. She would be a nurse, Olga a teacher.

All of the girls went to the Methodist college at Stamford at one time or another. When Olga went there in 1915, it was with the idea of doing preparatory work that would make her ready for a teacher's college. She did her two years at Stamford, taught country schools for a year or two, and was ready to go away to the Denton Normal School, later North Texas State University.

The summer before Olga was to leave for Denton was also the summer the rains came. They began in early August and kept on into September. The skies were dreary for days at a time, and when they parted to let a little sunshine through, it would be but a day or two before the clouds came over and the drizzle began again. The earth absorbed until it was saturated, and soon there was no place for the rainwater to go. It ran in the ditches and stood in the crop rows, made the roads slippery and the fields swampy. The farm people mostly stayed inside, except for the necessary chores and essential trips to town.

There was a wire wheeled Dodge in the car shed, but it was far too wet to get it out when it came time for Olga to leave. Mart hitched the wagon to a team of mules and loaded Olga's trunk on the wagon bed. On a day when the clouds hung low but the rain had stopped, they drove east up the road and turned north at the corner, drove past Bob White's house and past the Dixon place, and on toward Anson. Olga would catch the Wichita Valley to Abilene, then the T & P to Fort Worth.

Not so far out of Anson, the mules bolted and broke into a headlong run. Helter skelter they went, Olga hanging on and Mart trying to rein them in. The wild eyed mules galloped a half mile before bouncing the trunk off onto the roadbed and into a ditch. When everything had settled, Olga's things lay strewn across the muddy road and over into the ditch. The trunk lay open in the mire, spattered inside and out. Mart and Olga picked up the dresses and hats, books and underthings, and piled them in the wagon. When they arrived in Anson, Olga laid over an extra day to wash her clothes and clean and repack everything before going on to Abilene, Denton, and the rest of her teacher training.

Olga would later teach for over thirty years at Oak Knoll School in Fort Worth. She took special delight in the visits of her nieces and nephews at rodeo or circus time. As an aunt, she was unsurpassed. She had the biggest legs, the kindest eyes, and the warmest hugs that the children could have known. Whenever Olga visited brothers or sisters where there were children in the house, there was always some surprise for each one—a tin of candies, a new piece of clothing. Olga had a way of making each one feel especially favored.

Olga spent many summers on the home place, both before and after Mart's death. Whenever she was home again, Mart exercised the authority that, in his mind, was always due a parent in relating to a son or daughter. When Myra could no longer manage after her years alone on the home place, she lived with Olga in Fort Worth, and continued to take an active and vocal interest in Olga's comings and goings. Olga took care of her mother as long as Myra lived. By the time she was ready to retire and enjoy her travels, Olga had cancer.

In their relations with Mart, John and Olga were as different as any two people could be. As the fourth child and the oldest boy, John also grew up in the early years, before experience had mellowed any of the stubbornness out of Mart. John thus grew up in the path of some of Mart's early and inexperienced efforts at child rearing. The result was a relationship that grew crossways, and with the personalities and circumstances as they were, the split never mended.

All through his growing up years, John was as much a part of the family as any of the others. He did his farm work, bantered with his brothers, joined in when there were good times on the Clear Fork. When World War I came about and the United States entered to fight, John went to the Navy. He served on the high seas and fought on the U.S.S. Georgia. He made his way in an outfit that did no pampering, came through shipboard training and naval battles to return home safe. When John came in home, he was twenty-four years old and changed.

Mart had expected that John would settle down, make a farmer, and marry some good Jones County girl from a good, church going family, and he was ready to help his son make a start in this direction. Mart turned the one hundred acre Truby place over to John and sent some of the younger boys to help him work it.

John never really farmed, but he "farmed at it." His

interest was not in the land, but in good times and lively female companionship. John was restless for a more free rolling way of life. Plowing and hoeing just didn't make it anymore. Mart saw the half-hearted job of farming, the distractions and frivolousness and craziness in which John indulged. There was nothing he could do about it, but Mart had not learned that yet, so he tried to set his boy on the straight path the only way he knew—by telling him what to do and what not to do.

By the end of the one year on the Truby land, John had lost whatever interest he ever had in farming in Jones County. He turned the land back to his father and drifted north to Burkburnett, then southeast to Breckenridge. John worked in the oil fields some, followed the girls, kicked up his heels when he felt like it. When John came home, Mart aired his disapproval, and the more Mart pressed him, the more John didn't come home.

One morning while Haskell Caffey readied himself to go to the field, his Uncle Mart turned in up the lane and stopped in front of the house. Mart was going to Breckenridge and needed extra tire casings to have along against the possibility of a blowout. Since Haskell's car was of the same model as Mart's, he had the right spares in the shed and was glad to loan them. Mart drove away to Breckenridge and said the things that he wanted to say to John. After that time, John never came home again. He drifted again, south to Mexia, then farther south to Mexico.

John wasn't heard from for years at a time. The other sons and daughters grew up and left home, and still John didn't come back. A neighbor told Myra about the Veterans Administration and about benefits that she would be entitled to if John had died. By writing the V.A., she might at least learn whether John was living and she might learn where he had gone. Myra wrote the letter, and in a few weeks came a reply providing an address for John in San Francisco. Myra wrote several letters to the address and received two letters from John before he lapsed into silence again.

When Olga made a trip west, she went looking for her brother at the San Francisco address. Instead of a house, she found the V.A. office. In 1953 came the news of John's death. The one tie that John had maintained from his days at home was his membership in the Masonic Lodge, and it was through the lodge that the message came. Rudolph flew west from Denver for the funeral.

It wasn't as though Mart wanted to hold his children on the farm. He looked to education to open the way to other opportunities more attuned to the changing times. Mart was satisfied to see Wiley and Rudolph go off to Simmons Academy for courses that would get them into college. He was proud to see them go into Simmons College. Mart sometimes would take one boy or the other to flag the train at the Wichita Valley crossing after a visit home. When one of the boys needed just a little help to stay in school over a dry spell, Mart loaned him the money. When Wiley went broke after his years studying at the colleges in Abilene, Mart let him farm the Truby land for a year to make some money that he could use for the completion of his studies.

For awhile the growing up years made no very noticeable difference around the home place. The work went on as usual, the grown girls were in and out frequently, and there were always plenty of boys around to keep things in an uproar. Sula married Ned Welch and they settled on Mart's land near Truby. Olga taught around at several of the country schools before finally moving off to stay. Bonnie and Viola worked close by too, until they married.

It was getting on toward the twenties when things began to change. Bonnie married Ivo Stephens, who worked for the railroad. When he was transferred to Missousi, Bonnie went too. In December, 1918, came the word that Bonnie had died. The winter had seen the spread of a strain of influenza more terrible and deadly than any within memory. The pregnant women were especially vulnerable, and, at twenty-six, Bonnie was suddenly gone, and with her the grandchild that would have been the first for Mart and Myra. Bonnie had been an extraordinarily good person, a favorite of family members, a favorite of neighbors and cousins.

The news of Bonnie's death came at midday, with Mart and Myra working around home and the younger children down the road in school. At this time Olga was one of the two teachers at Elliott schoolhouse, and Wiley was boarding away at Simmons Academy in Abilene. When Mart and Myra had been told, Mart called down to the Rice place and Mrs. Rice walked across the road to tell Olga at the schoolhouse. The news set the schoolroom in an instant ruckus of shock and grief, Olga broken up beyond consolation. School was turned out for the day. When the news reached Wiley at Simmons Academy, he could hardly find a way to believe that it was real.

Bonnie's body was to arrive in Anson by rail. Mart and Myra and all of the brothers and sisters put on their Sunday clothes and drove to town to meet the train and have the funeral. But the body did not arrive as it was supposed to, and they had to go back home and come again the following day. When the body did come in at the platform in Anson, the casket was taken off the train and hauled to a private home for the funeral. Then a trail of autos followed the hearse carriage pulled by two white horses—through town and out along the road east, toward the gentle knoll of Mount Hope Cemetery.

It came to be expected that each of the sons would in turn make the short journey to study in one of the colleges in Abilene, but Wiley's decision to go off to Austin and study law represented a more radical and permanent departure from the home place. At that distance, there would be no weekend visits home, and maybe no coming home for Christmas. When Wiley finished he would not be a Jones County country boy anymore, but a smooth dressing city lawyer. Mart raised no objection, but Wiley didn't wait around for goodbyes. By leaving quietly Wiley could avoid the sentimental farewells and at the same time sidestep a lot of advice that Mart would surely bring forth on the occasion of his leaving. Wiley chose an afternoon when the family had gone to town to pack his case and take his departure from the empty house. He left a note on the dresser and walked out to the road to catch the first of several rides that would see him through to Austin.

By the mid-twenties, Mart's family was thinning. Wiley was in Austin at the University of Texas. Rudolph was away at school too. Olga had moved on, and only Viola and the younger boys were left around home. By now the country boys were being sent to Anson for their last school years, so each in turn, Boyd, Dalton, and Glenn went to town each day instead of boarding away at Abilene as the older brothers had done. When it came time for Boyd to go to Anson High School, his widowed Aunt Piney was living on a corner across from the school. Boyd rode a horse to town each day and turned it out in Piney's lot. At noontime he walked over to feed and water the horse. In a matter of months, Boyd and Viola had gone in together to buy a 1924 Model T, and thereafter they made the drive together, Boyd to study and Viola to work.

After finishing at Anson High, Boyd went on to Hardin-Simmons College. Dalton did the same in his time. Boyd and Dalton both graduated from Simmons, then took jobs in small town schools. Viola married Joe Ward and set up housekeeping in Anson.

By 1935, only Glenn was left at home, and that only because the Depression had temporarily put an end to his studies. Glenn had been away to college in Abilene already, and would have stayed straight through except that he ran out of money to continue. Having gone broke in a time that offered no ready opportunity for working, he returned to help at the home place.

With fewer of his own sons and daughters around home to help in the field, Mart had come more and more to depend on the Mexicans who came looking for work chopping cotton in summer or picking in the fall. Each year the ragtag camp of the cotton pickers moved in at the edge of the pasture behind the barn, and as the years went on, the Mexicans came to make up almost the whole field crew.

Still, if one of the boys was at home on the farm, Mart expected him to be among the rows with the rest of the hands, handling a hoe or dragging a cotton sack. It may have been that Mart could keep on feeling that all was well and he was in control of things as long as he had sons laboring under his direction.

This insistence on Mart's part brought him into a mild state of conflict with Glenn in the youngest son's last solitary years at home. The events of these months also revealed the mellowing that had taken place in Mart—that had reduced him from a rigid authoritarian to a man who accepted his own mortality and who could lose an issue to one of his boys without erecting a wall of rancor.

Having once left the farm, Glenn had taken with him the happy thought that he had pulled his last cotton boll. Glenn had never cared much for the field work anyhow, and as brothers and sisters had grown up and left, the work lost whatever fun there had been when there were good companions to share the hours with. Glenn would not for a minute, at Hardin-Simmons or in any of the days after, long for his days of chopping and picking. Now suddenly back home, pressed to get into the field and get a move on, Glenn could not put himself back to the time when Mart's command sufficed.

Glenn was willing enough to do his part. At picking time he supervised the field crew and did the weighing. When Mart was gone to the gin pulling a load of cotton behind the car, Glenn stayed in the field on the wagon, taking the cotton sacks as the hands brought them in full. He weighed the sacks, read the scales, made note of each hand's production, dumped the sacks into the trailer. So it wasn't as though Glenn was idle. Still, Mart wanted to see him out among the rows pulling bolls as the sons and daughters had always done. Every few days in picking season during Glenn's last two years on the farm, he was asked the same question: "Glenn, have you bought your cotton sack?" "No, I haven't got around to it yet." Three or four days would go by and Mart would ask again, "Glenn have you got that cotton sack yet?" "No, Papa, I haven't got it yet." Glenn never did get around to buying the ducking material for his sack either of those years, and Mart never got around to confronting him directly with the issue. By 1935, Glenn had picked his last cotton and Mart had reached the end of the days in which his boys could be buffaloed into unquestioning obedience.

When times improved some and Glenn began to plan for the resumption of his studies, Mart was having second thoughts about seeing his last son leave the place. Mart was well past sixty, and he ws needing help to handle the farming anymore. Besides, if Glenn stayed on he would have a ready made occupation and a chance to take the place over and continue to operate it as his own someday. Glenn was not much inclined to the idea, and his older brothers and sisters had been urging him to get on away from home and get back in school. When the harvest had been finished in 1937, Glenn began to make his arrangements for enrolling in Hardin-Simmons for the coming spring term. Shortly after the first of the year, he was packed and gone. When Mart did his plowing and planting in the spring of 1938, there was for the first time in thirty years, no son to help him see the crop through. The sons and daughters were all on their own, and so was Mart.

*   *   *

For a time, Wiley, Dalton, and Glenn lived under the same roof in Abilene. Wiley had always been one to help a family member in a time of temporary need, and there were plenty of those times in the Depression years.

Wiley was still a bachelor at thirty-six. He had settled in Abilene to pursue his legal career, and was off to a good start. After a beginning year with the venerable partnership of Cox and Hayden, Wiley had struck out on his own, and now was Abilene's City Attorney. Having experienced enough of hotel and boarding house living, he had bought a frame house on North 16th. Dalton was working toward graduation and supervising the demonstration school at Hardin-Simmons, and he had recently taken a bride. He and Estelle moved in to share the house while Dalton worked on toward the end of his college days. When the Depression eased and Glenn could leave the home place and return to school, there wasn't the money to pay for a room in Ferguson Hall, so Wiley took his youngest brother in too.

The arrangement was, for the most part, a satisfactory one, all except for the few times when Wiley's set ways ran head on into the more free-wheeling styles of the younger boys. Such an occasion presented itself early on when Dalton made a habit of driving up out front and pulling his car right up into the yard, so that it struck a defiant pose a few feet from the front door. Wiley regarded this practice as a sign of low class, and he chastised Dalton severely, letting it be known in no uncertain terms that the cars at this house henceforth were to be parked in a conventional manner—in the driveway or along the curb.

When Wiley bought the house, it came without a mailbox. This made him no difference, because he didn't get his mail at home; he got it at Box 204 in the post office downtown. When the kinfolks moved in, they naturally gave out the house number as their mailing address and thus brought about the need for some receptacle for the postman to deposit letters in. The problem was mentioned to Wiley, but he somehow never got around to taking care of it. He kept meaning to, but it was not the kind of chore that came natural in his daily routine. Finally Dalton took the initiative and solved the matter himself. Being a practical sort of man, he took a cigar box and nailed it up to the wall on the front porch. When Wiley saw the result of Dalton's work, he was not pleased. Within a day or two, Wiley found time to get to the hardware store, and he came home carrying a respectable looking mailbox that was promptly mounted by the front door.

171

Wiley held certain ideas about proper hygiene that stayed with him always, that he always took seriously whether others did or not. After once finding a dead fly in the bottom tip of an ice cream cone, he decided that it was unsafe to eat that last small point of the cone; when his children came along, they were taught accordingly. Whenever he was served potato salad, Wiley wanted to know when it had been made; he had once come down with food poisoning from leftover potato salad.

One of his habits was to take a glass off the shelf and turn it up to inspect it before getting his drink from the kitchen faucet. Perhaps this quirk was learned from a lifetime of living in houses where dust sifted in from the outside and where bugs were relatively free to wander through the kitchen. At any rate, Wiley wanted to know that the glass was clean. It was to be expected, then, that he took this notion with him when he went into the kitchen to get a drink one evening before leaving the house for a date, dressed in his finest new white suit. He went to the cabinet and took a glass from the top shelf, turned it up to look inside, and found himself showered with tomato juice that Estelle had put back to use later. It was during these months that Wiley's own characteristic slow burn expression was first invented.

Bed slats must have been among the things that God made in order to keep people from taking themselves too seriously, for there is hardly a family that cannot relate some tale of mishap involving bed slats. Wiley had his own experience during the time that he shared a double bed with his brother Glenn. The house was sparsely furnished, the pieces mostly second hand. When Wiley bought the bed, it came with slats that were too short to reach across from one siderail to the other. The previous owner had ingeniously tacked a strip of leather to the short end of each slat, and then to the siderail of the bed, so that the combination now reached all the way across and supported the bedsprings. Lacking either the inclination or the aptitude for things mechanical, Wiley had never bothered to improve on the makeshift arrangement.

Wiley took a more-or-less paternalistic interest in Glenn's doings in these his young brother's early years away from home. It was because of this that Glenn crept quietly when he entered the house in the early hours one morning after a longer than usual night on the town. Glenn got out of his clothes in the dark, then considered the problem of getting to his side of the bed with Wiley already asleep in the other. With his own space wedged between Wiley on one side and a wall on the other, Glenn started up over the end of the bed, putting his arms out front of him one after the other, as though the mattress would sag any less because his weight was held high instead of low. Glenn had inched to the head of the bed, let his weight down, and gone limp with relief, when every slat fell out of the bed and crashed to the floor. With the mattress tilted askew and both men rudely jarred into a state of confusion, Glenn found the switch and turned on the light to find Wiley sitting up startled, blinking his eyes and wearing a towel around his head turban style, the way he always did when he had just washed his hair and wanted to avoid taking cold from exposing his wet scalp to the cold night air. The slow burn was on again, as Wiley got to his feet and went about setting the springs and mattress level again, humming a line that made no recognizable tune, but that served to contain his irritation.

There is no telling what havoc Glenn and Dalton might next have wreaked on their older brother, had Pauline Marlin not suddenly and permanently come into his life, causing their eviction from the house on North 16th.

11. Five Cent Cotton

All through the 1920s the Jones County farmers went along enjoying a period of relative stability and prosperity. After the disastrous "Twenty Break," cotton prices had partially recovered and had drifted steadily upward to levels of twenty, twenty-five, and even thirty cents a pound—not the wonderful peak prices of the war years, to be sure, but enough to provide a comfortable living nonetheless. While people around Jones County weren't getting rich, many of them could afford to live in good houses and drive new cars and share in the newest comforts and conveniences of the day. Fences stood straight and taut along the country lanes, shiny black autos were commonplace, and except for the tenant shacks, there was good paint on the houses.

Actually, it may not be quite correct to say that the farmers were "enjoying" the favorable market conditions; few of them could realize how well off they were. Some of the farmers even then groused and grumbled that they were not receiving their fair share of the nation's ever increasing wealth. Many others took the good conditions for granted and saw no reason to doubt that their lives and fortunes would continue at the same level and even improve. Little did they suspect that shattering changes were so near.

All through the twenties, even as farmers were pushing production and cashing in on the favorable market conditions, gradual and imperceptible changes were gnawing away at the underpinnings of the cotton economy like termites at a wooden bedstead. With one good jolt, the whole decimated structure would come crashing down.

Over the decade, a vise-like pressure began to squeeze the small cotton farmers. On the one hand, demand for farm products was slowing down. During World War I, many European countries had been unable to produce adequate supplies of food and fiber themselves, so had welcomed huge quantities of American exports. With their own producers recovering in the early twenties, these countries adopted protective policies and raised barriers against American products. At home cotton farmers faced new and formidable competition from the developing synthetic fibers. They did not welcome the appearance of rayon fabrics.

On the other side of the squeeze was the ever more troublesome problem of overproduction. With more and more cotton being produced and demand slacking off, prices were bound to suffer sooner or later. During the bonanza years of the first World War, Mart had cleared new patches of shinnery and rushed new acreage into cultivation to take advantage of the extraordinary prices paid for cotton. With thousands of farmers across the country doing the same, many thousands of acres of new crop lands went into production. Even as demand for cotton was tailing off in the twenties, these new lands continued to produce. In fact, with improved farming methods at work, almost all croplands were producing like never before.

New technologies helped to compound the problem of oversupply. By the middle twenties, several Jones County farmers were hauling loads of cotton to the gin behind autos instead of in horsedrawn wagons. All across the country, other farmers were doing the same, making greater use of trucks and automobiles, and later, tractors. At first glance, this use of power equipment would seem to be a wonderful advantage for the small farmer—it made the hauling go faster, saved labor, made farm life a little easier. But an unfortunate effect of the massive switch from mules and horses to motorized vehicles was a further inflation of cotton production and another step toward the inevitable price drop. With fewer work animals needed for farm chores, farmers kept fewer horses and mules. Acres that had previously been used to raise feed for these animals now came to be used for the production of crops for market. More than twenty million acres were shifted from feed crops to money crops over the decade from 1920 to 1930. With demand for cotton falling and production rising, the squeeze closed in on cotton farmers. By the last years of the decade, their livelihood was in a precarious condition.

The imminent break in cotton prices was delayed and masked only by a sort of artificial propping up of the demand, and hence the price. With times generally prosperous over the twenties, people had money to spend, and consumer goods moved at a pace unseen in any prior time. People didn't eat more than before, at least not much more, but they enjoyed new gadgets and appliances, filled closets and dressers with clothes. This higher-than-normal level of consumption, combined with the reckless speculation of the last months before the crash, served to hold cotton prices up when a drop was long overdue.

There was one more problem to complicate the lives of farmers as the slide approached. With farming on the upswing and crop prices enviable in the early years of the 1920s, farm land had been an attractive buy and farming an attractive occupation to young men starting out. Consequently, farm land had brought handsome prices and there had been many sales. Because of this, a good many farmers now were laboring under the burden of heavy mortgage obligations. They were safe as long as prices held, in jeopardy if prices were to fall.

A calamity of any kind was far from Mart's mind as the days warmed and planting time approached in the spring of 1929. The whole country was riding the crest of a period of unprecedented economic growth, and while farmers may have been losing ground relative to other segments of the economy, their lives, too, were getting richer and more comfortable. Cotton prices, though somethat lower than the decade-high level of 1923, were holding plump and steady, hovering at twenty cents a pound over the previous two seasons.

Mart listed up the land and planted from fence row to fence row. Through the hot summer days, maize and cotton plants came up and leafed out, grew toward maturity and harvest. Mart ran the cultivator up and down the rows, hired Mexicans to chop the weeds out. By mid-August, he laid the crop by and looked forward to selling at prices better than any before.

As speculation was driving stock prices skyward through the summer months, so too were commodity prices on the rise. By the time Mart had his cotton in, prices had been bid up beyond any Jones County had seen before. Mart finally had twenty bales to sell and was offered an incredible forty-five cents a pound. Such was the bouyant optimism of the times that farmers had reason to believe prices would go higher still. Mart held off selling, determined to sit tight and sell at fifty or even fifty-five cents a pound.

When the crash came in late October, cotton merchants began to suspect what was becoming clear to others: that prices were far overextended, that the real prospects for demand and consumption hardly justified the prices they had been paying for raw cotton. With manufacturing in decline and an abundant supply of cotton on hand, demand plummeted. The pattern of times to come was not yet clear, so Mart watched and waited for reversal while cotton fell to thirty-five, thirty, on down past the good levels of the twenties, down to an unthinkable pittance. Mart saw the market hit bottom, waited until it was certain that there would be no recovery, sold his twenty bales at five cents a pound.

Despite the sudden and calamitous drop in prices, the cotton economy didn't disintegrate all at once. Rather the small farmers did their best to hold on, in hopes that their fortunes would change—that a normal recovery would restore prosperity and sustain a way of life that had gone on for generations. There was no immediate end to the era of quarter section farms, large families, and small country schools and churches. Rather this arrangement of people and institutions endured years of slow and painful strangulation. Ultimately the old way was beyond rescue, for too many things had changed too drastically.

Farmers did their best to weather the slide. Most of them had little choice in the matter. With production winding down in all sectors of the economy and millions out of work in the cities, alternatives did not exist in abundance. Dismal as the conditions were, a family stood to survive as well on the farm as anywhere else, for there at least were the means for producing food and fuel. While the twenties had generally been a time of migration from the farms, this trend now stalled and even reversed. Just as Glenn retreated to the home place when the slide caught him in his college years, so did other families gather to the sustenance of the land when other sources failed.

If a man owned his land and had some money saved up, as Mart did, he could get by all right. Otherwise, the family was apt to lose everything. After the break of 1929, it would be five years before cotton prices rose above the still paltry level of ten cents a pound. Successive years of six and seven cent cotton separated the sheep from the goats, sent the washed out families to town while solvent ones stayed on the land and clung to what they had.

Even with the pitifully low prices paid for raw cotton, production increased to an all time high in 1931. There was no ready means by which thousands of individual cotton farmers could act together to limit supply and drive up the price. Each farmer could only seek to maximize his income by planting more acres and harvesting more bales, so the supply problem got worse instead of better. Each spring the farmers would plant again, always hoping for the recovery that would bring a decent price for the crop by fall. When the improvement failed to materialize, farmers struggling to service mortgages were left short. Cash reserves were soon swallowed up in expenses and mortgage payments, so that many farmers were left at the mercy of their creditors. For some, the process of going broke was painfully gradual, drawn out over years of alternate hope and despair.

For many Jones County farmers, the power to make or break lay in Joe Steele's bank—the First National of Anson. While across the country banks were wilting by the score, the First National remained solvent—partly because of Joe Steele's hardline policy on foreclosures. While others went broke, he made out all right, taking in land and property right along as notes went into default. Some of the country people came to feel that the man didn't have a heart.

Some of the farmers lost land to the bank, and some had never had any to lose. For a tenant farmer or a farmer who had lost title to his land to the bank, Joe Steele would write a note against the man's crop, livestock, and implements, and loan him a few hundred dollars to live on through another season. A farmer might thus go along from year to year, digging the hole deeper as long as his credit held, until finally ruin or rescue would settle the issue. If there was somehow money enough to keep the bank satisfied at the end of a season, the family might get by. If not, Joe Steele's crew would come calling and haul the whole works off to Anson. Equipment and work animals were sold for whatever they would bring. Cattle were driven to holding pens beside the Wichita Valley tracks on the east side of town. There they awaited shipment, sometimes so full and crowded that they could hardly stir.

Over the months and years that the slide dragged on, the depression settled in over Jones County, seeped into its lifeblood and gnawed at its bones. In Anson, conditions deteriorated steadily over the years when money became ever more scarce. By 1932 houses were dilapidated and rattletraps far outnumbered the few new autos. In March of that year the Palace Theatre closed, gone broke from months of heavy operating losses. Streets and sidewalks crumbled for want of repairs, businesses on the square were bare and bleak for want of the bustling trade they had known in the twenties.

Anson collected a residue of despair, of displaced and destitute tenant farmers and of transient families stalled on futile cross-country migrations. There was a good bit of drifting during the low years, especially as dust bowl droughts drove farmers broken and defeated out of Oklahoma and parts of Texas. Some went to California and some just drifted. Some landed in Anson and huddled in shacks by the railroad tracks. Some finally left and some were too poor to leave.

The penniless drifters and the local poor got by on private charity, on scavenging, and on rumors of impending developments that would ease their miserable lives. A few were driven to the edge of desperation.

One evening a little before closing time, a man walked along the square and turned in to Rosser's Grocery Store. He said nothing to anyone, but walked straight to the bakery shelf, picked up two loaves of bread, and walked out the front door with them. Mr. Rosser made no move to stop the man, but instead followed him down the sidewalk and trailed him at a distance. The man walked south off the square and stepped along the rutted back streets. At a plain little crackerbox house the man turned in, entered and let the screen door slap shut behind him. The grocer followed to the door and peered into the room, where a half dozen urchins gorged themselves on ragged hunks torn from the loaves. In moments both loaves had disappeared. Mr. Rosser turned back toward town and went about his business.

Within a couple of years of the crash, the home place had begun to show signs of neglect. Mart had never been one for unnecessary spending, but now he was more cautious than ever. With neighbors going broke all around him, Mart nursed his reserves, doled out small sums only when essential goods could be had no other way. He bought some clothing for the family, a little gasoline, seed for crops. New economies exposed the wear and tear of hard times. Downed fence wires didn't get repaired or replaced as before. Worn implements were patched up and used another season when before they had been discarded for new ones. The old barn was crumbling, but Mart had to make do with it. When paint cracked and peeled from the house, Mart let it go. An early casualty of hard times was the phone system. With country people unable to pay for its upkeep, the line was abandoned, the phone sets unfastened and taken to town.

Living on your own stuff—that was how the country people got by. They mended and re-mended what clothing they had, learned to put cardboard in the soles of their shoes where holes had worn through. Some homes backtracked from kerosene stoves, resurrected the old wood burners and began hauling stovewood again. Except for basic staples, all food was produced at home or gained in barter with neighbors. For meat there was chicken from the back yard or ham from the smokehouse. Families that had taken to buying canned goods in town now learned to garden in earnest, and to put up supplies that would last the year. Because Mart and Myra had most always lived frugally and worked hard, the depression times showed them few hardships that they had not experienced sometime before. Others had never learned to rawhide it, so they were hard put to fend for themselves. Some resorted to unusual tactics. Mart was surprised one morning when he walked down to the lot to do his milking as usual, only to find that someone had already beaten him to it.

In the first three years of the depression more than five thousand banks failed nationwide. Joe Steele's bank never folded, but Mart didn't wait to see. When he had heard enough of surprise closings and lost savings, he went to town and drew out his money, kept out enough to live on and buried the rest in a fruit jar. Mart's family didn't lose any money in the bank failures, but they knew neighbors who did.

When Mrs. Rice died, John Rice sold out in Jones County and went to farm in Arkansas. Two young sons were left to be raised by Menco and his wife, now farming just south and west of the old Rice place. When John Rice died in Arkansas, none of the children could get away to go and sell the property and settle the estate. Menco corresponded with a Holiness preacher who had been John Rice's friend. Preacher King sold the land and implements, deposited several thousand dollars in the bank at Mena, Arkansas. When the farming season was finished and Menco could travel to see about the estate, the bank had closed. Over the next two years Menco kept writing to the bank's receivers, getting back letters promising that all depositors would be paid. Finally came a check for forty dollars and a letter telling that this would be the final settlement of the account.

By the end of 1932, Jones County farmers had seen enough of Hoover's "New Era." Franklin D. Roosevelt carried Jones County by 2339 votes to 180 for Hoover. Farmers watched to see what Roosevelt would do to bring their lives back to normal. In the early months of 1933 the new president made headway in stabilizing the chaotic banking system, but general economic recovery and improved farm prices were still well in the future. The farmers would struggle through more years of deprivation and discouragement while the government wrangled with judges and tinkered to urge the economy out of its paralytic state.

When things finally started to get better, they didn't get better very fast. By 1932 Menco Rice was living in Anson, having been forced from the land by the pinch of too many lean years pitted against too little cash and property. Four years later Menco was still working for fifty cents a day—running machinery at the gin through the fall and winter, working for the city in summer. When the new lake was finished in 1936, the city advertised for a pumper to handle the water system. Forty-nine men applied for the job. Applicants were invited to bid on the job, each one naming the pay he would accept if hired. Menco offered to work for whatever the city could pay, and he was chosen for the job, even over men who had said they would work for as little as forty dollars a month. Menco was paid sixty-five, along with the use of a house, phone, garden plot, and pasture for his cow. For Menco, the depression ended in 1936. For forty-eight others, it went on.

With the coming of the New Deal farm policies, the farmers learned to figure in a new factor when calculating their prospects. They had always watched seed, labor, and equipment costs, weather, and market conditions. Beginning in 1933, they also kept an eye on the government's farm policies, which would henceforth have much to do with their fortunes. New terms came to be commonplace wherever farmers gathered to chew over ins and outs of their business. There were acreage allotments and benefit payments, and subsidies for land that was allowed to lay out. The objective of the farm program was to control production, so that the gross oversupply was eliminated and the relative scarcity of cotton and other farm products would naturally lift prices to levels the farmers could live with.

The first Agricultural Adjustment Act became law just after spring planting, 1933. In order to make the production controls effective as soon as possible, the government paid farmers to plow under millions of acres of cotton already in the ground. In Jones County, some seventy-five thousand acres were plowed up, with farmers receiving around eleven dollars an acre for cotton so sacrificed. Jones County went along with the farm program, but the philosophical shift indicated by the new policies did not go unnoticed. The *Western Enterprise* took note of the occasion in front page commentary:

Many a farmer browned with years of labor
in the sun this week has had a new experience.
Monday the first cotton was plowed under after
the emergency permits had been granted . . .

183

Oh no! It is not the capitulation to the teachings of Eugene Debs that makes cotton raisers and producers 'kinda' sad this week. We can all stand the Government going socialistic, regardless of how much we believed in the old-time Democrat's theory that the Government should stay out of business, when it intercedes to save our hides. It was not the injury done to old political legends, therefore, but a bit of sentiment that prompts those expressions of regret on the part of many when they started the revolutionary project of plowing up perfectly good cotton from knee high to hip high, heavily burdened with fruit . . . But sentiment has to be discarded and politics forgotten when it comes to cashing in on a deal that means bread and meat to you.

In future years, government manipulation of market conditions and farm income became routine. For farmers who cooperated to stay within their acreage allotments, the government provided additional benefit payments. By the time war had powered the economy back to full throttle, a sizable government bureaucracy had evolved to administer the farm program, and a return of farm products to a free market system seemed remote. West Texas farmers, perennially threatened by drought and hail, were conditioned to scan the horizon daily in a constant vigil of hope. This they continued to do, but with the New Deal years and after, they learned to keep one eye skyward and the other trained on Washington.

*   *   *

Though it would take global war to finally bring the collapsed economy back to full employment and all out production, Jones County was slowly pulling out of the worst in the late 1930s. By 1936, telephone service had been reestablished in the shinnery communities. Not everyone could afford a phone this time around, however, so some of the struggling tenant farmers would walk up to Mart Caffey's or a neighbor's house to call out if a doctor was needed or a child was lost. With government payments now supplementing market income, farmers had a little more money coming in, so Mart could replace the dilapidated wreck that was his barn. By 1937, Glenn could think about leaving the home place to resume his college studies in Abilene. By 1938, Mart had the cash and the confidence to buy a new Ford. As the depression lifted, it left a different face on the old shinnerylands.

The hard times left Jones County with a good many shacks abandoned along the country lanes. Once the worst had passed, people left the farms as never before, most of them headed for the cities and towns, where wartime production was making jobs for all who wanted to work. For most of the departing families and for their descendents, there would be no going home to the farm. With new kinds of farm machinery coming into general use, one man could farm the acreage that had once occupied a half dozen families. With the help of trucks and tractors and mechanical harvesters and government support, a man could still make a living farming the larger parcel of land, but there was no place for the quarter section or eighty acre farm, and no need for a dozen children in each family to help with the hand labor.

With fewer and smaller families scattered over the country, attendance at the rural schools dwindled. In some communities a school building that once had rocked with forty or more pupils now rattled hollow with eight or ten. With enrollments down and school buses now in use, the country schools began falling like dominoes in a row. Elliott schoolhouse was already gone, an early casualty of the depression years. The others would follow—dozens of them—until the only schools in the county were in the towns. With the schools went also the rural churches, folding one by one as membership dwindled. When the

Unity Grove Church disbanded in the late thirties, neighbors in the Elliott Community began driving to the Baptist Church in Anson, or to the smaller one at Pleasant Grove.

Through three decades the country around the home place had been abundantly populated with good people—the kind that neighbors could count on. By the time Glenn left home, it was different. In the early years, neighbors had known one another, had joined together to provide for schooling and worship. They had shared each other's work, bartered food, shared in good times and family tragedies. After the depression, country people had less in common and less to do with one another. With fewer families scattered over the country and with the community schools and churches gone, people kept to themselves more than before.

In the newer times there was greater diversity among the rural people, less common ground. Still left from the old times were a few of the older couples, living on their same small farms and living as much like before as times would allow. The mainstream no longer ran past their front doors, but had instead moved to town, leaving them to the sounds of crickets and creaking windmills where once noisy children had kept up a constant ruckus. Still in the country, too, were some of the old time tenant farmers—ones who lacked the ingenuity or ambition to move on to city jobs that would have made them a good living. These were people who, for the most part, had been poor and would stay poor, getting along on odd jobs and day labor as the possibilities for small scale rent farming dried up.

The earnest farmers of the new age were of a different breed. They were younger men more concerned with efficiency than their fathers had been. The new farmers concentrated on their money crops, let slide some of the old chores and ways. They bought groceries in town, left off keeping hogs and chickens and milk cows. They paid more attention to the county agent and less to phases of the moon, more to equipment depreciation schedules and less to First Monday trading.

Finally, there was a new kind of country folk. Some of the older, smaller farms were bought by people who worked in town and wanted to live in the country, and perhaps to farm eighty or a hundred acres on evenings and weekends. In the new times, a man had to have a job to support eighty acres, because it sure wouldn't support him.

Mart went about his work on the home place, kept to the life he had made and let the rest of the world go on where it would. He no longer kept hogs and fed them himself, but as long as one of the boys was home to help with the butchering, he knew where he could buy one to bring home and dress. With the help of a tractor, he could go on making crops, hiring itinerant Mexicans to do what hand work there was.

After the worst wasting years of the depression, Mart never had the place shipshape again. Ten years of hard times and tight spending had left a legacy of wear and tear too extensive to be set back in good order in a few months or years, especially with the newer and more moderate standards of farm income. Weathered old farm buildings were left to serve where new ones were needed. Ragged fences were mended willy nilly, kept just good enough to contain whatever cows were on the pasture. There had been a time when Mart would have seen that the house had a new coat of paint every two or three years and new wallpaper when the old was cracked and faded, but Mart was almost seventy, and that time was past.

The depression left Mart more certain than ever that the best thing to do with money was to put it in the bank and not spend it. When cotton prices improved and Mart had money coming in regularly again, he was not much inclined to turn loose of it.

Myra came out of the hard times with a bitter resentment for the Republican party and a resolve never again to be taken in by the promises of a Republican. She had voted Democrat ever since women had gotten the vote, up until 1928. In that year, she had joined many others in believing Hoover's promises of a wonderfully prosperous age to come, and with those hopes dashed so miserably, she held him to blame. She had violated her own strict loyalty to the Democrats and it hadn't worked out. It was a mistake she would not repeat.

*   *   *

With his college years behind him, Rudolph had gone off to New York to find his making as a singer. He did well enough through the rough depression years, had regular work in theaters, clubs, and stage shows. He did night clubs on the east coast, fairs across the midwest, worked with Ed Wynn in Chicago. By the end of 1940, Rudolph had put together the makings of a career; he had contacts and connections and a name that was known in enough circles to keep him in one engagement after another. Rudolph had a fine tenor voice, and show business chums were betting he would go right on up.

Whenever personal tragedy strikes in a family, there often seems to be one member of the family who responds more quickly and more fully than the others, whether by compassion or by circumstance. When Mart was suddenly stricken with cancer, Rudolph was that person. When the word came, he closed out his obligations, packed his bags, and traveled for home.

Rudolph came in down the country lane, took on the brunt of responsibility for his mother and father, settled in to stay for the duration. He spent long hours at Mart's bedside in the front room, helped move and feed and tend him, watched in patient compassion while the disease wracked and wasted Mart. When the pain grew too violent, Mart was kept medicated to a miserable stupor. It was a bad time, but Rudolph stayed by, kept the house in order and buoyed his mother.

Sons and daughters came as they could. When Wiley

came from Abilene one morning, Mart called him to the bed and told him where to find the money he had buried out back. Wiley took a shovel and found his bearings, stepped off measured paces according to Mart's instructions—so many north from the corner of the house, so many west. He plunged the shovel into the ground and turned the earth. Before long, he had poked around and struck a solid object, crouched to uncover the stained old fruit jar. Wiley took the jar back to the house, wrestled it loose from its rusty lid, and pulled out a mildewed roll of bills—the old oversize bank notes that had not been circulated in years. Wiley took the money to the bank in Anson, walked to the window and set the clammy wad before the teller. The young man said nothing about the odd deposit, but peeled off the moldy bills and counted them out, glancing up periodically to wonder again at the man who could have presented so peculiar a cache.

One morning when Mart had been several days in a state of drowsy, senseless misery, the fog suddenly lifted and let him enter the present lucid and aware. When dinner time came Mart was too weak to move from the bed, but he called for Rudolph to carry him to the table. Rudolph lifted the frail body, carried Mart into the dining room, sat him in his chair at the head of the table. His strong voice weakened with disease, Mart turned his head and motioned slowly, deliberately, around the empty table. "Rudolph, this is your place over here. Wiley, this is your place. Bonnie's place was right here. Olga sits here. Viola used to sit here. . . ." In the afternoon the thick cloud settled back over Mart, put him back where no one could reach. On the thirteenth day of March, aged seventy-one years, Mart breathed his last.

*   *   *

When Rudolph returned to New York, the feeling of upward momentum and impending fame had passed. For a time Rudolph worked the old circuit, kept food on the table with performances on the trail of night spots and fairs. In the meantime, he also took an interest in real estate and began trading options on property in Florida. When the entertainment business was in slack season, Rudolph kept track of the real estate market; when state fair season rolled around, he took to the road again. Rudolph was up north working one of his regular gigs when a phone call came from his wife in Florida. May had good news. "What am I doing here?" Rudolph said, "Why, I can make more money on that one piece of land than I'll make here all year." Rudolph wasted no time in moving on the opportunity. As soon as he could pack, he was gone south. Rudolph would take to the road again many times in the years to come, but not as a singer. Instead he would range over Florida, Colorado, and Texas, taking in the country and dealing in houses and businesses, ranches and farms.

With the war on in earnest, Myra's family was scattered far and wide. Glenn was off to help mop up in northern Africa with the Army Air Corps and the other sons and daughters were working in scattered places. While they made new families and homes, Myra went on with her own life, fed her chickens and kept her garden, read her books and listened to the night sounds of the quiet shinnery country.

12. Uncle Fletcher

One of the few remnants of old times around the home place to survive into my childhood was Uncle Fletcher. The other brothers who had come from Mississippi were all dead and gone, their families scattered and their lands mostly sold away into other enterprises. Myra still lived alone on the home place, but Mart was long since dead and the children all out and away, well into their own different lives and careers. Some were nearing retirement themselves. The land on the home place was rented out to Bogus Lollar, who made the crop and paid Myra a third of what it brought.

At this time, in the mid 1950s, Uncle Fletcher was into his eighties, a character and a curiosity. He always had been that. Uncle Fletcher lived on a little shinnery farm that was as scruffy as he was. The pear orchard had been let go, though it still produced some good fruit. The buildings and pens had not been maintained in years. The little shed of a barn was weathered through from all sides, the pens a jumble of half-rotted posts and broken down boards. Weeds and underbrush threatened to take the place over, and Uncle Fletcher did nothing to interfere with the process.

Most times when we drove down the dirt lane toward the home place, Uncle Fletcher was sitting out on the little "L" shaped porch that was set into the front side of the house under long, shading eaves. The house had been painted white at one time, but that was a long time ago. So narrow were the ends and so steep the gables that the little house had an almost vertical appearance about it. It was a somber sort of place, shaded in the Texas sun, hid-

191

den away down a little lost road from a world speeding by only a few miles distant.

My father and I often stopped to interrupt the time that Uncle Fletcher spent there on the small porch, alone with his thoughts. Sometimes my father pulled in of his own accord, other times because I begged him to. The women in our family did not share my fascination with Uncle Fletcher, so we hardly ever stopped when they were along.

He was like nothing else in my world, this weathered old character with long, bristly moustache, full grey beard, and scrappy old clothes—the old man from the sticks, who stayed to himself except for occasional trips to town, who walked or was picked up on the road everywhere he went. One of the oldest pictures in my mind is of Uncle Fletcher walking out through the field across from his house, coming out of the pastureland and headed toward home, driving eight or ten cows ahead of him with a crooked stick.

Uncle Fletcher was the last of the four brothers—the last one born, the last to come to Texas, the last one laid in the ground on the low rise east of Anson. He was different in other ways too, from his brothers and from most everyone else around Jones County.

Uncle Fletcher never wanted to come to Texas, never fully gave in to it once he had come. Fletcher would have been just as glad to have stayed back in Mississippi, in surroundings like the ones he grew up in. The slow turn of progress, the confinement of the small parcels of farmland, the resignation to a simple life—these were things that the others had wanted to get away from, but they suited Fletcher just fine. They left him at peace with a world that made few demands on him. He probably *would* have stayed too, had it not been for his brothers and their cajoling him to follow them to Texas.

As long as either of his parents was living, Fletcher stayed in Prentiss County to look after them. Months after his father had died, Fletcher's mother sent a note to the county clerk's office: "Please let my son have a marriage license." Fletcher, several months shy of twenty-one, married Mary Hamilton, and together they lived on the old family farm with Nancy. When Mart and Edgar came home after Nancy's death, they exhorted Fletcher to come back to Jones County with them. There was nothing more to keep him in the old country, and besides, the youngest brother had always been the sort that needed a little looking after. Better that he be near his brothers. At his older brothers' insistence, Fletcher became the reluctant pilgrim. Mary stayed behind to sell the property and settle up business, then followed west.

Fletcher never lived like the other brothers—never shared their inclinations, their gregarious ways, their view to the future. He took up farming on an eighty acre place that was way down in the shinnery and far from any road. It was accessible only by taking a wagon or riding a horse and following the fence rows through a succession of fields and pastures. The dust blew and the sun sweltered on the forgotten backwoods farmstead. Only a two room shack provided shelter for Fletcher and Mary. There they lived and worked, scratching a living out of the forty or so acres that were in cultivation. They lived much the same as they might have lived in Mississippi, resigned to a meager existence and prospects for more of the same.

Sometime while he and Mary still lived in the backwoods, Fletcher went through a rough spell, his behavior growing steadily more ornery and erratic as the weeks passed. Old man Hestand had been going around over the country buying up mineral rights, trying to put together a fair sized oil lease, which he finally did. He had been at Fletcher to sign into the deal, and, true to character, Fletcher was not interested. Mr. Hestand continued to pester Fletcher, trying to change his mind, and Fletcher was rankled at the infringement. When finally, in a fit of temper, he picked up a rock and hit Mr. Hestand in the head with it, Fletcher was taken in hand by the sheriff and sent off to the state mental hospital at Wichita Falls.

After a time, Fletcher had had enough of the place.

Without waiting to be discharged, he walked off to make his way home. Traveling by night, he stopped at farmsteads along the way, stalking up around the house to see what he might find. Around back at most of the places was a screened-in milk cooler. Fletcher would drink his fill, then steal away into the night to continue south.

Word of Fletcher's departure from the mental hospital drifted back to the Elliott community and to Anson. When night fell over the country with Fletcher expected to turn up at any time lamps burned at farmhouses scattered over the country, the neighbors frightened of Uncle Fletcher. Mart and Myra and the younger boys were off on a trip, two others of the brothers and sisters taking refuge at a neighbor's house. Only Wiley was at the home place.

Far up into the night, Fletcher walked the last dusty stretch and came up into the yard. "Is that you, Uncle Fletcher?" Wiley called out. It was. Fletcher had been to his home down in the shinnery, found it deserted. Wiley told his uncle that Mary was living in town—he could go there tomorrow. Wiley got up to make a place where Fletcher could lay down and sleep the rest of the night, but no, Fletcher said that he was too dirty to sleep in a bed. He wrapped himself in a quilt and slept on the floor.

With Fletcher back around town, people started complaining. They knew he wasn't supposed to be out of the mental hospital. So Fletcher was sent back, examined and judged sane, released and sent home to stay. Fletcher and Mary soon bought a fifty acre piece of land connecting with their original place and fronting on the road a half mile north. They moved back to the country and resumed their farming.

Fletcher and Mary grew some cotton, but their main product was fruit—mostly pears and blackberries. To raise cotton, a man had to break the land, plant the seed, and chop away the weeds and grass that threatened to sap water and soil nutrients, then get the crop picked and hauled in the fall. This routine entailed keeping mules or horses,

194

maintaining plow and harness in good repair, hiring and bossing laborers. All in all, it was a lot of work. If no preparations were made, no cotton grew. If seed was planted and then left untended through the growing season, the field grew up in Johnson grass and careless weeds. With the pears, it was different. With spring came the blossoms and summer the small fruits. By fall there were pears. Bad weather might spoil the crop, but there was not much a man could do about that. By and large, the whole process of pear growing could be left up to nature, and this was more to Fletcher's liking. Oh, there was trimming and weeding to be done, but Mary was a hard worker, and she made sure things were right with the orchards and bushes. As for Uncle Fletcher, he didn't take to work too much.

Mary was about the only civilizing influence in Fletcher's life. As long as she lived, he stayed bathed and shaved and had clean clothes to wear. And while Fletcher was never really in the mainstream of productivity and progress in Jones County, he wasn't so far out of it either—wasn't the social drop-out that he became later.

Like his brothers and most of the other neighbors, Fletcher was a religious man. He and Mary made most of the neighborhood church meetings, and Fletcher studied his Bible during many of the hours in which he was neglecting the farm work. There was a pump organ in the house, and it often poured forth the strains of old hymns that had come from Mississippi. Fletcher made all of the rural singing schools and singing conventions, and once made up his own gospel song that came to be published in the song book edited by R.H. Cornelius. Fletcher's song was about the great star of the first Christmas night: "Guide me home, home above, to that home of love. And it led men worshipping to the presence of the King; Holy light, still abide."

Fletcher had committed a good many scriptures to memory, and he often interpreted the events of the day-to-day life around him in terms of biblical passages. Not far from Fletcher's place lived a lively young ruffian—Ralph Shirley. Ralph was a likeable old boy, but his goodtiming ways often led him into trouble. Ralph worked at his brother's gas station in Anson during the day, spent his nights in carrousing and roughhousing. He drank a little too much, and was ready to fight with only moderate provocation. People told Ralph that he was headed for trouble if he didn't take hold and change his habits, but Ralph wouldn't listen. He kept on living free, kept on ending up in minor scrapes and predicaments.

Ralph ran with a fairly rough group of characters, and among them was a fellow who was sometimes a sort of rival to Ralph—Cecil Hunter. One evening the rowdies were having a time on a street on the east side of Anson. In the course of things, Cecil backslid into a state of drunkenness and passed out on the curb. Ralph was white enough to take the boy home, but not enough to open the door before stuffing Cecil in the car. Ralph just picked the limp body up and heaved him in through the rear window, glass and all, cutting Cecil up in the process.

In time Cecil recovered, and he nurtured his grudge against the one who had roughed him up, biding his time until he should have his opportunity for revenge. One afternoon he happened to hear that Ralph Shirley was shooting dice in the back room of a cafe in Stamford. Cecil took a singletree to the blacksmith shop and had the heavy metal clips taken off it. With the singletree in his hand, Cecil walked in on the game and knocked Ralph Shirley in the head and killed him. When Uncle Fletcher heard what had happened, he quoted from the Proverbs: "He who is often reproved and stiffeneth his neck shall suddenly be destroyed, and that without remedy."

From his school days, Uncle Fletcher remembered the great authors. He admired them, and sometimes liked to try his own hand at writing. Fletcher wrote poetry, epigrams, essays, and stories. When he died, sheaves of yellow pages were left in the faded little house.

Fletcher was somewhat the philosopher. He

ruminated at length on the great questions of life, drawing on the Bible and other works with which he was familiar for ideas out of which to forge his own principles. He turned thoughts over and over, searched out threads of insight, issued conclusions on the most fundamental mysteries of life and death. A few days before Christmas in 1922, Fletcher took up his pencil and wrote on the tablet—a poem and then two of his own proverbs: "Our greatness in Life will be determined largely by our attitude in Death." . . . "Physicians do not cure me. They only scourge me & still I must Die at last."

Fletcher and Mary never had any children, a fact that set them apart from most all of their neighbors. Large families were the general rule, and many of the country women seemed to have one child after another throughout their childbearing years. Fletcher had a way with kids all right; he seemed more at home with Mart's boys than with his own brothers, but he and Mary remained childless.

For all that she did to hold the place together and brighten his threadbare life, Fletcher yet wanted it clear that it was he, and not Mary, who ruled the roost. Mary's was a solitary life at times, her days passing in desolate places with only the moody Fletcher for company. Once when Fletcher and Mary were together at the house back in the shinnery, a wagon rolled toward their house from the south. On the seat were Bill McCoy and his wife, the nearest neighbors that Fletcher and Mary had. They owned the adjoining farm, one even farther down in the shinnery than Fletcher's. The McCoys had driven up for a friendly evening visit, and Bill reined the horses to a halt before Fletcher's porch. Mary was glad to see the visitors and she urged her husband to make them welcome. "Fletcher, why don't you invite them in?" she implored. Fletcher wouldn't have it. "Woman, you hush," he scowled, putting an end to the discussion and the visit.

On another day, an insurance salesman happened up the road, making the rounds of the country places. Had the man known Fletcher Caffey, he surely would have passed the place by. Since he did not, he stopped to make his usual pitch, hopeful of making a sale. The man made his small talk, then began to explain to Uncle Fletcher about the benefits of life insurance. He told of how it would help Mary later on. Uncle Fletcher considered the matter, then rendered his point of view in his own slow talking way: "Well, now . . . you know, . . . I don't remember ever promising to take care of Mary after I die." The man closed his case and went on his way.

Fletcher had little more use for banks than for insurance salesmen. His inclination was to distrust them, so Fletcher sometimes did his own kind of banking—with a shovel, out in the orchard. Once when Menco Rice delivered a calf for sale, Fletcher had him wait at the house. Fletcher took off back toward the orchard and returned a short time later with the calf's price in mouldy bills.

Uncle Fletcher was a man of few words, but the things that he said often reflected a good deal of forethought and subtlety. He had a way of making a remark that would seem to go unnoticed, only to ferment in the listener's mind and provoke some insight later on. One day Edgar's boy, Haskell, a grown young farmer at the time, came to Fletcher's place to buy a bushel of fruit. As was the custom, Haskell took his basket to the orchard to pick his own fruit. When Haskell returned to the house to pay, the basket was heaped high, so that pears threatened to topple to the ground if Haskell failed to step carefully. A great mound of fruit came over the rim of the basket, extending far above the bushel measure. Fletcher noticed the unusual load, but made no effort to confront his nephew directly. "Oh well," he said as Haskell took his basket, "I suppose some folks is just naturally greedy."

Even with his eccentricities, his backward ways, his lack of ambition, Mary was crazy about Uncle Fletcher. She stayed with him through everything until she died in 1939. Mary's funeral was at the Methodist church in Anson, the church a silent and hollow place, vacant but for a few relatives and one lonesome wreath that one of Mart's boys had brought from Abilene.

After Mary was gone, Fletcher became even more the eccentric, the recluse, the oddity of the backwoods. During the seventeen years that he lived on without Mary, Fletcher grew away from her influence, and the times outside his backcountry world went off and left him for good. Fletcher inevitably became a character—an embodiment of the odd and unexpected and inexplicable in human nature. The house and barn began to run down, the orchard grew up in weeds, the berry patch went to ruin. The old pump organ, now relegated to the barn, was ruined by the weather, ravaged by mice. Uncle Fletcher still ran a few cows, picked a few pears—did just enough to keep a little money coming in, just enough to occupy a few daylight hours.

Otherwise, Fletcher did as he pleased. He often walked the dusty miles out to the main highway that ran between Abilene and Anson, walked along one way or the other until some neighbor picked him up. Fletcher had never mastered the art of driving a car, never got the hang of it. He had tried a few times in earlier years, but always seemed to end up tangled in a tree or mired in the sand. The one time Fletcher had ventured to own a car, the relationship didn't last long. One morning soon after the purchase, Fletcher was loose-herding the old Nash down the lane toward his house when it left the road out of control and plowed into a row of tin mail boxes mounted on posts, sent them flying with a terrible clatter. At the moment of disaster, Fletcher happened to come face on to the rear view mirror where he saw, as he told it, a sky behind him "raining mail boxes." Thereafter Fletcher had walked or caught rides.

On Sundays Fletcher sometimes made his way to the men's Bible class at the church in Anson. Fletcher knew the Bible by heart, and was contentious to the point of irritation whenever he felt that Mr. Connell's teaching ran afoul of the Word. Fletcher stopped shaving, got along on clothes he already had, wore the same shirt for days between washings.

Uncle Fletcher could hardly be persuaded to eat outside his own house. Left to fend for himself, he often boiled up a pot full of eggs and ate off them for several meals, until they were all gone. He would stay for dinner at Sula's house over near Truby, but nowhere else. When Myra's children and grandchildren gathered for a family Christmas at the home place, Fletcher always waited until dinner was over, then came walking up the road to visit on the porch for awhile. One year Glenn took Uncle Fletcher a cake on his birthday. It was freshly baked, but Fletcher put it away and left it alone, not only while company was there, but for days after. In a few weeks Glenn stopped in again to find Uncle Fletcher enjoying a piece of the cake, now hard and stale, in a bowl with milk over it.

Finally the years came for Uncle Fletcher. When he knew that he could no longer take care of himself, he sent word to Sula to come and take him to the hospital in Anson. Sula and Ned appeared at the house in a day or two and loaded Uncle Fletcher and a few possessions in the car. The house was left just as Uncle Fletcher had lived in it. As they drove through Anson, Uncle Fletcher asked to stop at the bank. Mr. Warren came out to the car and showed Fletcher where he had money, a thousand dollars or so, and with the satisfaction that his bills would be paid, Fletcher was ready to go on to the hospital.

Once bedded down in the new, one-floor rural hospital, Uncle Fletcher was contrary and unmanageable. Dr. Duff, who had found Fletcher so amiable when he had picked the old man up on the road to Abilene, could do nothing with him now. Uncle Fletcher wouldn't eat. He wouldn't let the doctors examine him. He refused to let the nurses so much as take his blood pressure. He wouldn't even consider standing in front of the X-ray machine. He was cantankerous to the nurses, recalcitrant before the doctors. He drove them all to frustration. They had never had a patient like Uncle Fletcher. Fletcher straightened up only when one of his nieces or nephews came in to visit.

Day by day the old man grew weak and thin, stubborn in his resolve to spurn all efforts at meddling with his infirmity. When doctors tried feeding him through his veins, Fletcher pulled the needle out. Finally Uncle Fletcher turned his back on the bothersome figures in white, his face to the bare wall. Far from his Mississippi home, he died.

13. The March Winds

I was born in 1947, in time to know the home place in its last years. I was the youngest of all Myra's grandchildren—Wiley's little boy come along late, after it had looked like it would be just him and Pauline and the two girls. I was no more than seven years old when Myra moved off to Fort Worth, but those few years before then let me into an era I would not see again.

It was ritual in our family that Friday evenings were spent at the home place. After school was out and my father was home from work, we loaded in the car and headed for Jones County. More often than not, we stopped at a market and bought a good piece of round steak to take along. We drove the twenty miles of highway, turned off onto the country lane, and left a trail of dust as we rolled toward the home place, three miles down the road.

Myra greeted us on the porch, then set to cooking supper. If we had round steak, she took and pounded it with a churn lid, floured it, and threw it in an iron skillet. And if there was no meat, she went into the back yard and grabbed up a chicken off the bare ground, gave a quick twist to the neck, and had its head off and the thing dressed and in the pan before you could say scat. My mother once suffered a traumatic ordeal when Myra had given her a live chicken to take home and cook. Her rearing in Methodist parsonages in Hannibal and Denver had not prepared her for the task. She approached it with dread, which proved to be justified when she began to wring the bird's neck and had it, amid much flapping and squawking, escape her grasp and run wildly about the yard with its neck stretched and dangling and the job only half done. The experience left her with a resolve never to accept such a gift again, and with images that years later could give her the willies. To Myra it was nothing—just one of the dozens of little daily chores that came with putting meals on the table.

Myra at seventy-eight wore a wry smile through her wrinkles. Her hair was put up in a tightly wound bun on the back of her head, the way she had always worn it. The years had stooped her some, but not enough to keep her from her usual farmstead chores. Myra went about her days in peace and looked forward to the occasional visits of grown sons and daughters and their families.

The home place was much as it had been over the many years, though it too was showing wrinkles. The weathered old car shed leaned wearily to the right. It still housed a 1938 Ford, the last car Mart had bought, but Myra didn't drive, so it was hardly ever out. Whenever one of the boys was home on a visit the car was started and the engine run enough to keep a charge in the battery. The house, once new and freshly painted, now was showing its age. The porch steps were worn down smooth on their edges, the paint on the walls cracked and peeling from long exposure to the Texas sun and sand. Window screens were bulged and patched, and here and there a strip of molding flapped loose. There was still no plumbing at the house, though two of the grown sons had recently built a new one-holer out back. Water still came from a tank that caught rain off the roof by the kitchen, and from the cistern at the side of the house.

Myra still put in a garden, still did her canning. Mason jars of beans and peas and preserves and chow-chow were stored in the dank underground cubicle that sagged a little more each year. Myra still found a garden snake in the cellar now and then, killed it with a hoe. There were cows in the pasture, but they weren't Myra's. They belonged to a neighbor man who paid a few dollars to run them there. In summer Myra could still look to the east and watch the leafy green cotton plants growing up in rows for as far as the eye could see. The field work that had once been done by Mart and the boys and hired Mexicans with hand tools now was done mainly by Bogus and a tractor and the various chemicals and gadgets that had come to be accepted accoutrements of farming. After the years of daily demands involved in keeping Mart and the family fed and clothed and straightened out, Myra answered only to herself. Now there were no cotton sacks to be stitched, no squirming heads to be combed. Myra was at peace with her solitary life—had settled into a few comfortable habits that gave her pleasure, like her snuff and the romance magazines she liked to read.

On many Saturday mornings my father and I made expeditions to Jones County. Seldom was the Saturday that I did not come out of bed at daylight, ready to start in on my father about a drive up to the country. On most weeks he could be brought around without much difficulty, responding with a "Maybe" that meant we would go. After a stop at the post office and perhaps an errand at his office in the red brick Taylor County Courthouse, we were gone.

These were good times for both of us. In season we walked out into the field to inspect the cotton plants and to recall the boll fights of bygone days. Often we explored the wooded pasture, forging through the mesquite, post oak, and underbrush, sometimes reaching a place called "the glade," an open, meadow-like space that included old piles of car parts, cans, and bottles. Sometimes we came out to the far fenceline and crossed over into Dixon's field, and walked around the well and foundation that had once made a family home. Occasionally we walked down the road from Myra's house to cut a long, tassel-topped cane from the cane patch that stood at the bottom of a shallow draw. Sometimes we navigated the rough, narrow lane down to George Elliott's place to visit and buy a dozen eggs fresh from the hen house. George and Nora, both well up in years, lived in a small house on the east end of the old Elliott land. George recounted the old days in a loud wheezing voice while Nora leaned forward to hear what was said, and to put in her own piece with the louder than necessary tone of a person grown hard of hearing. If my father could be persuaded, we drove home along the river road, beside the shaded, overgrown Clear Fork, where the Caffey boys had fished and picnicked.

With the passing years, the Elliott community became ever more sparsely populated. The houses and families that had occupied each 80 or 160 acres in the early years now were nowhere to be found. Here and there plain little shotgun houses sat weathering away, sun sifting in through their perforated shingles, winds whistling through the cracks and hurling tumbleweeds in through the paneless window frames. Every few years another house was abandoned, the field left to some farmer who had bought or rented the property to add to other crop lands. Long overgrown were the plots where Elliott Schoolhouse and Pleasant Hill School had stood. A newcomer to the country could not have known that there had ever been a building in either place.

There were a few real farmers around over the country, men who kept a yard full of equipment and worked tracts of land several times the size of the old farms. Along the country lanes there were still scattered houses where an older couple or widow remained on the old place, not because it was still a viable enterprise, but because it was home. The open country, once in motion with children playing and hands at work across the fields, now usually was solitary and silent except for the mechanical groan of a lone tractor in the distance.

Only at Christmas was there traffic on the roads and motion around the houses. Christmas brought them back—the pupils of Elliott and Pleasant Hill, the cotton pickers and egg gatherers and wood cutters, the riders of ornery calves and the dodgers of cotton bolls. Wherever they had gone, however far they had grown from their young days on the farm, at Christmas they came home driving new cars and bringing mates and families.

When school let out for the holidays, Olga came to

help her mother make ready. By Christmas day, all of the sons and daughters and grandchildren and in-laws had arrived, overflowing the house. All but John. A dozen or more cars sat at haphazard angles off the road, not just at the Caffey place, but at other old family farmsteads over the country roundabout, places where one or two now remained in a house that had once held a whole brood.

Myra's house would not contain the hubbub; it spilled out onto the porch and into the yard, ran with the grandchildren down the road to the cane patch, followed them on explorations back into the pasture. There was no way for feeding the whole gathering at once. Instead the children were fed first, then as many grown-ups as would fit around the table in the middle room, until all had eaten.

In Myra's living room was the old upright Mart had brought home for the price of a wagon and team. Beside it hung the pictures of Wiley and Rudolph with the Sans Souci Glee Club, and one of Boyd with his quartet at Simmons College. Sometime after the dishes were cleared away, my mother was called to play for singing—old hymns, Christmas songs, songs of the range, popular songs of the forties and before. Glenn sang his Irish songs, Wiley his sacred favorites, Rudolph the crooning songs from his days in New York. Boyd and Dalton and Glenn harmonized on "It's a Treat to Beat Your Feet on the Mississippi Mud," as they had done at functions around Jones County in earlier years. Myra rocked and listened.

All day long, along with everything else that went on, there were stories of the growing up years, some familiar from repeated tellings, others recalled from out of the blue—stories about Uncle Edgar, about Mendel Elliott, about Eldridge Lipham's antics in an old Model T, about the load of wood stolen from Bob Carter's woodpile, about Viola's line in a school play. By sundown most of the families had set out for home, their socks grimy with the feel of Jones County sand in their shoes.

After Christmas Olga went back to school and things

returned to normal. Myra read her books, fed her chickens, put on a black dress and hat each Sunday when Sula came to carry her to the Methodist church in Anson. The countryside lay quiet roundabout, only rarely interrupted by the sound of a car or pick-up raising the dust on the lane out front. Now came the colorless days of late winter, the field bare and brown, the shinnery a grey mass of bare branches. Darkness fell early over the shinnerylands, and when it did Myra could usually be found rocking before the butane heater in her front room, rocking and reading.

Before long came the winds of March, and with them sand that swirled from the earth and was hurled across the prairie from the north. Myra hated the dust storms. Sand sifted in under the door and swept across the linoleum. It came in through the cracks in the windows and left the sills brown and gritty. It clung to her skin and scalp, settled between her toes. When the brown clouds blew, nothing was impenetrable. With their coming each spring she swore to leave the place before the season rolled round again. But no, when the pink sky rose over north each year, Myra was still there.

Finally, with their mother approaching eighty, the sons and daughters persuaded Myra to move off the place for good—to go live with Olga. What triggered their insistence and her consent was a spell Myra had one afternoon when she was at the house alone. Mysteriously, Myra's head fell over and she was left weak and dizzy, unable to help herself. Myra crawled to the telephone and dialed Sula's number, but could make no words when Sula answered. Sula hurried over in the car, got her mother going again, took her home to her own house.

In a few days Boyd came from Vega and took Myra to a doctor in Amarillo. She was examined and found to have myasthenia gravis, a disorder of the nervous system, producing sudden weakness and fatigue in the muscles. The doctor perscribed medicine that Myra would take for the rest of her life. Myra suffered no serious harm from the incident, but it was clearly time that she should be moving to where there would be someone to look after her.

The move to Fort Worth was to be made during Olga's Christmas vacation. After one last family Christmas, Myra's belongings were packed and readied for moving. The piano, the treadle Singer, and most of the furniture would be left behind.

On the morning of departure, the fields of the Elliott country were white with six inches of snow. The bare mesquites and post oaks were trimmed in white, and the heavy winter sky hung low over the shinnery. Icicles decorated the fence wires and eaves.

Glenn and Ruth came from Abilene to help with the move, holding fast to the roadway and away from the bar ditches as they drove the last stretch up the country land. Myra's things were loaded into the two cars, Olga's and Glenn's, and the little caravan crept away up the road east out of Jones County, out of the shinnery, and away to the city. The year was 1954, sixty-four years since Mart and Myra had first set foot in Jones County.

To Wiley fell the duty of looking after the farm. He made the deals with Bogus when it was time to lease the land again each year before planting season. He kept the house up, found men in Anson who would make occasional repairs as they were needed. He kept the house rented, went to the *Western Observer* office to place a new ad whenever it came vacant. Our Saturday trips began to include short stops to see the renters, more critical, proprietary looks around the farmstead. We checked the old barn and lot occasionally, stopped to talk with Bogus whenever we found him plowing or met up with him on the road.

Myra took to her life in Fort Worth far better than anyone had supposed she would. For awhile she and Olga tried returning to the home place on weekends, but that didn't last long. Myra took up air travel and found it to her liking. She made long summer trips to stay a week or more with each of her children, flew to stay with Boyd in El Paso and to see Rudolph in Denver. Myra liked television and found the afternoon soap operas entertaining in the same way that her romance stories had been. Her favorite program of all was "The $64,000 Question."

The house on Westbrook was surrounded on the back and sides by a deep ravine that put other houses away at a distance. The ravine grew full with tall trees, shrubs, and vines. In fall, the brown leaves settled over the earth in a crumbling organic blanket. Leaves drifted up knee deep in the low places. The surroundings were easy on the eyes, and Myra could be happy in the years that she rocked and read in her back bedroom while Olga was away at school.

Myra lived to eighty-four, took sick out at Sula's house in 1958, on one of her summer visits. Before she could get better in the hospital in Anson, she took a fall and broke a hip as well. Myra lasted a few days, died, and was buried next to Mart and Bonnie at Mount Hope.

It was left to my father to settle the estate. He worked at the chore for a few years, until each separate task had been taken care of. There was no hurry in closing the estate, but neither was there any sentimental reluctance on his part. It was simply the next thing to be done—it was what came now. He took charge of the bank accounts, paid off bills and expenses, corresponded with insurance companies. He took the will to be probated, administered the distribution of the proceeds among his brothers and sisters. He paid the taxes and collected on outstanding obligations. When the time came to put the farm up for sale, we went to a musty office on the square in Anson, next to the Pittard Drug Store on the corner, and listed it with old Mr. Littlefield.

Mr. Littlefield put ads in two or three papers, told the farmers he knew about the Caffey place that was up for sale. Several people around the county were interested enough to talk price and have a look, and before too many weeks a deal had been struck. The sale went through in the early months of 1963.

Rudolph called the law office one morning, ready to

put down his money and keep the farm in the family, but he was too late. Charlie Owen was the new owner. Charlie was an amiable fellow, a stocky man who had started with a small place near Stamford and bought up parcels around him over the years, so that his holdings now were considerable. He paid sixteen thousand dollars for the Caffey place, worked the land himself, and continued to rent the house out as my father had done.

None of the brothers minded seeing Charlie Owen have the home place. Charlie was a capable farmer and a good man, one who had put down roots in Jones County and worked for everything he had right there. He was known and well thought of across the county. When we drove by the home place occasionally and asked whether we might walk up into the pasture, Charlie was always glad to oblige.

Charlie Owen had worked the place only three years when he fell dead of a heart attack. The farm was sold again, this time to two recent G.I.s who had moved into Abilene, worked in town, and wanted to live in the country and do a little farming on the side. They went in on the farm together and used their veterans' loan to put up the price.

The week before one of the new families was to move into the house, it burned to the ground. A modern brick home, one with plumbing and automatic heating, was raised in its place. The farm was split down the middle by a new fence running the breadth of the place north and south, so that each of the new owners now had half a field. The man who had bought the east eighty dozed a space out of the shinnery along the road that had run north and south along the far end of Mart Caffey's place. In what had been the back of Mart's pasture, he made a clearing and moved in a trailer, dug a well and strung a power line.

As the cedar fence posts came down around the periphery of the field and pasture, they were replaced with the thin steel fence staves that more of the farmers were using now. When a new fence was built along the road, it went all the way up to the edge of the yard, so that there was no longer a gate where before we had driven through past the windmill and up along the fenceline beside the field. The creaky old windmill was taken down and replaced with an electric pump. The car shed was leveled and the boards piled for fireplace kindling. The weathered old stable was abandoned, a new shed of corrugated iron built up closer to the house. The two weekend farmers began to run their crop rows north and south instead of east and west. Mart's crops had never done much good that way.

The new owners got the idea that the pasture didn't yield enough grass for grazing with the shinnery growing over it so thick, sapping the water and shading the ground. So they killed out most of the trees and cut back the underbrush, leaving a broken line of spindly mesquites where once a dense tangle of woods had bounded the field. Where a pasture had stood full and green behind the field on the north and west, making a welcoming view for anyone driving in home from the east, it was now possible to see through the few trees that remained—to see across to the other farms beyond the fenceline, and to the far north horizon.

Before very long, the home place was changed beyond recognition. Time took the old buildings, the old ways, and the people who had experienced their lives in the fields and woods around the shinneryland farm. Even so, not everything was different. In summer the fields baked in the noonday sun and bright sunflowers grew up in the ditches. In the fall crops were harvested and the stalks were left to be taken back into the bare soil. Winter days passed, and with them the bleak skies and chill mornings that were natural over the bare sticks of the shinnery. In spring the winds came as before. The northern horizon turned the color of new leather, and the sands of the home place swirled skyward and south.

Notes on Sources

A book of this sort necessarily entails major contributions by persons other than the author. It is only through the mass of impressions and recollections generated by those who knew the times firsthand that such a story can be assembled at all.

Most notable among those who helped provide the substance of the book are Glenn Caffey, my uncle, and Merle Caffey Haag. Glenn drove over the Elliott country with me and shared his experiences with me on several occasions, always bringing in some new and colorful tale, each one recalled in lively detail. He also read through the manuscript and made comments that helped make the narrative more complete and accurate. The early background of the home place and of the earlier series of migrations to the frontier could hardly have been sketched without the benefit of Merle Haag's genealogical research, a product of some twelve years work on her part.

Many others contributed stories or important bits of detail. Among these are Sula Caffey Welch, Boyd Caffey, Dalton Caffey, Haskell Caffey, Pauline Caffey, Jean Caffey Lyles, Nancy Caffey Smythe, Tim McCarter, Menco Rice, and Sammie Bennett.

The files of the *Western Observer* of Anson, Texas, were laid open to me through the courtesy of Homer Hutto, Editor, and Jerry Wallace, Publisher. Also included in this archive were the paper's forerunners, the *Western Enterprise* and the *Jones County Observer*.

Several books were particularly useful as sources on the historical context of "the old home place." Notable among these are:

Bernard Bailyn, et al., *The Great Republic*. Lexington, Mass.: D.C. Heath and Company, 1977.
Lester V. Chandler, *America's Greatest Depression*. New York: Harper and Row, 1970.
Katharyn Duff, *Abilene . . . On Catclaw Creek*. Abilene,

Texas: The Reporter News Publishing Company, 1969.

Homer Hutto and Hooper Shelton, *The First 100 Years of Jones County, Texas.* Stamford, Texas: Shelton Press, 1978.

Rupert N. Richardson, Ernest Wallace, and Adrian N. Anderson, *Texas The Lone Star State.* Englewood Cliffs: Prentice-Hall, Inc. Third edition, 1970.

C.H. McKennon, *Iron Men.* Garden City, N.Y.: Doubleday, 1967.

The following people provided photographs for use in the book: Leta Byrom, Dalton Caffey, Pearl Caffey, Merle Haag, Sue Vincius. Other photos were discovered in the barn when the home place was sold.

4644 144